P9-BYP-228

Sunset

WOOD CARVING BOOK

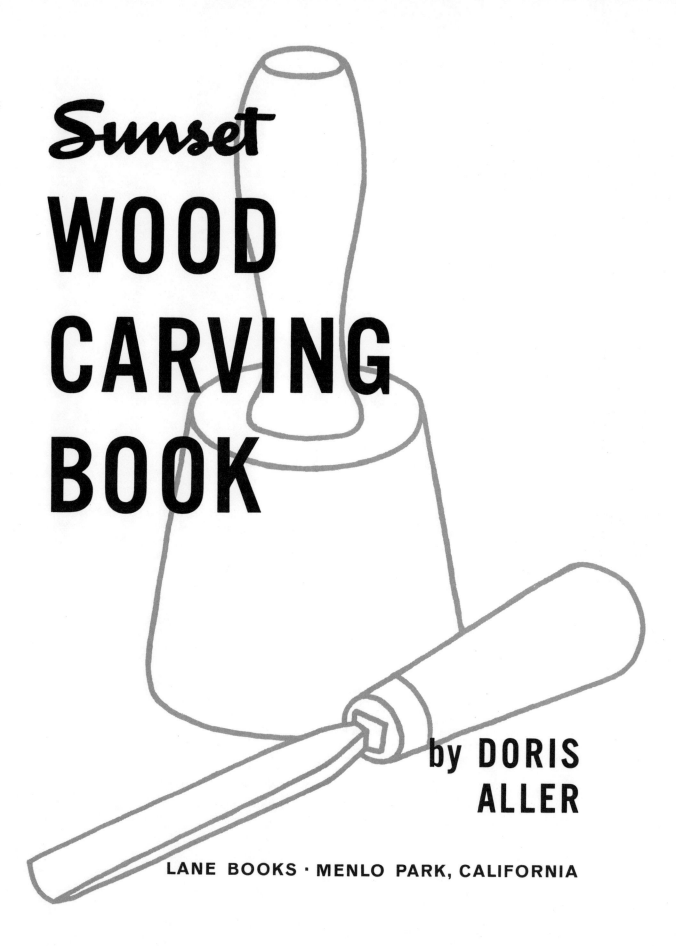

Sunset
WOOD
CARVING
BOOK

by **DORIS ALLER**

LANE BOOKS · MENLO PARK, CALIFORNIA

NOTE: *All projects appearing in this book except No. 7 were first published in* Sunset *Magazine.*

All rights reserved throughout the world. This book, or parts thereof, may not be reproduced in any form without permission of the publishers.

Library of Congress Catalog Card Number: 51-13032

First Edition

Fourteenth Printing April 1969

COPYRIGHT© 1951

LANE MAGAZINE & BOOK COMPANY, MENLO PARK, CALIFORNIA
By the Publishers of *Sunset* Books and *Sunset,* The Magazine of Western Living
PRINTED IN U.S.A.

FOREWORD

The first purpose of this book is to provide complete self-instruction for the beginning wood-carver. Pictures and diagrams are here to make each step plain. If you are without wood-carving experience and must "start from scratch," this book is for you.

Although many projects designed to be copied are included in this book, its second purpose is to stir the creative impulses of the carver and lead him to design original work. If you aspire to do wood carving either as a craft or an art, this book is for you.

A further purpose of this book is to present the carving of wood as more than a pleasant pastime or as a reflection of quaint decorative notions of the past. It presents carving as a means of forming useful objects with decorative qualities. If you want to make such carved objects for your home, this book is certainly for you!

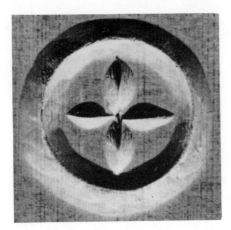

CONTENTS

WOOD CARVING FOR MODERN LIVING 11

TOOLS, ACCESSORIES AND THEIR CARE 14

BASIC CARVING TECHNIQUES 18

SUGGESTIONS FOR PRACTICE 25

HOW TO DO INCISED CARVING 28

Projects using Incised Carving

    1. Knife Holder 36
    2. Cup Shelves 36
    3. Dustpan Flower Shelf 38
    4. Butter Molds 40
    5. Serving Plank 42
    6. Marriage Chest 44

HOW TO DO CHIP CARVING 46

Projects using Chip Carving

    7. Garden Seed Box 48
    8. Desk Box 50

CARVING IN RELIEF 52

    Projects in Relief

       9. Case for an Oilstone 54
      10. Spoon Holder 54
      11. Book Cover 56
      12. Herb Box 57
      13. Carving Tool Chest 58
      14. Fireplace Bellows 60
      15. Jewel Case 62
      16. Garden Wheelbarrow 64
      17. Dower Chest 66

CARVING IN THE ROUND 69

    Projects using Carving in the Round

      18. Wood Spoon 74
      19. Spaghetti Forks 74
      20. Serving Dish 76
      21. Salad Set 77
      22. Whittled Scoop 78
      23. Wooden Dipper 79
      24. Polenta Scoop 80
      25. Wooden Doll 81

DESIGNS FOR CARVING 82

WOODS FOR CARVING 86

FINISHES FOR CARVINGS 89

WOOD-CARVER'S WORKBENCH 93

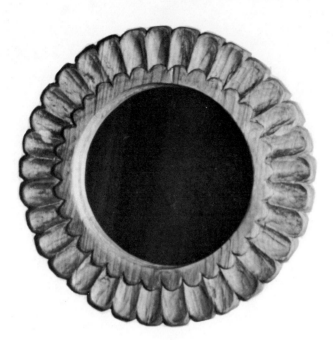

Carve to produce useful and
practical objects for the house.

Modern interiors make excellent
backgrounds for carved masks.

A shallow redwood bowl is a
pleasant bit of wood carving.

Wood Carving for Modern Living

Regardless of age or circumstance, few of us are so serious or purposeful that we can do without play. Further, we all possess creative talents. While these vary in kind and degree, they are instinctive in all human beings—a valuable part of our natural endowment. Therefore, when we can find an appealing activity that we can do "just for fun," at the same time allowing us to use our natural talents, we add much to life and living. We call these leisure-time activities—the play which has no connection with the duties, obligations and exacting demands made on us in the larger phases of our lives—"hobbies." In these pages we consider wood carving as a present-day hobby; moreover, one which will enable us to make our surroundings more pleasant.

No one knows when man first discovered he could shape wood, either for his pleasure or to make a better spear or tool handle for his use. We do know that wood, a friendly, natural material, has provided an outlet for the creative energies of man throughout his history, as well as providing him with an easily available, easily worked material with which to make needed utensils. A love of wood persists, and today as in the past a great many men, women and children find the carving of wood a satisfying and personality-rewarding hobby.

Is wood carving for you? If you seek an interesting way to use a little leisure time, if you enjoy using your hands and have the wit to tell one end of a chisel from the other, it may be

11

that it is. Happily, anyone with a desire to do wood carving will usually have the ability to do so, since the steps in the work are natural and easy to do. There are no arbitrary standards of achievement to discourage the beginner. Instead, there are many types and kinds of carving to provide scope for all degrees of skill or talent. This is readily seen when it is realized that wood carving includes the shaping of a simple bowl as well as the hewing of a monumental sculpture—that the texture imposed on wood surfaces, which is also wood carving, may be mere chisel marks in rhythmic repetition or richly modeled motifs. The end product of the wood-carver may enhance a cathedral or add charm to a kitchen!

Whether you carve something for your home, a toy for a child or a present for a friend, you will soon discover that the mild exercise and mental relaxation that accompanies the act of carving is conducive to the release from the tensions built up by everyday frustrations. If you are a man whose business is exacting, you will appreciate the freedom from strict demands of accuracy since wood carving doesn't call for such. Women usually find they have more free time as their children grow up and go away to school or to homes of their own, and often it is only then that they discover the pleasures of a hobby such as carving. However, the wise mother develops interests in hobbies for herself before then and also encourages such interests in other members of the family. Children old enough to use tools enjoy the simpler forms of wood carving.

The beginner often asks, "What should I carve?" There are a number of simple projects in this book which should answer this question, at least in part. They were all planned for homes, gardens and patios in the belief that what we carve should be considered in the light of how we live and that the greatest pleasure in wood carving is gained when the carved piece is one that can be used in everyday living. To this end, consider your needs and the way you live. Do you have a garden? If so, add a carved hanging lantern, a shrine, sturdy benches or flower boxes. Outdoor dining calls for wooden bowls, dishes, serving accessories and trays—many of these may also be used indoors unless your table is very formally set. The most efficient kitchens can be made more charming with the addition of a few homey wooden utensils. Wooden toys are fun to make as well as fun for the children's play. If you intend to build or remodel, plan carved architectural details—doors, a mantelpiece, or carved ceiling beams. Occasional pieces of carved furniture, such as chests or cupboards, are extremely pleasant in contrast with the simple forms and natural surfaces of much modern furniture. Modern interiors, because they are plain, make excellent backgrounds for wood sculptures, carved masks, picture frames, bookends and covers,

A large book cover is decorated with all-over pattern made by repeating two motifs. Wood is cedar.

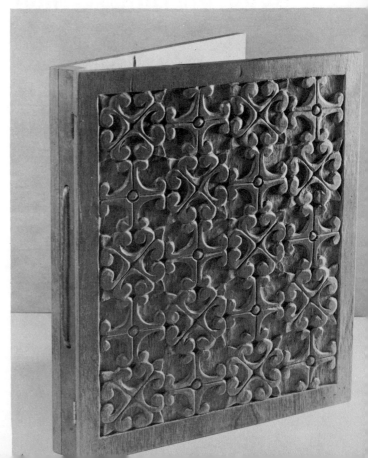

Carved incised lettering is appropriate decoration for personal treasures such as this— a daughter's marriage chest.

lamp bases and many more household accessories. Our first goal as modern wood-carvers should be to produce useful and beautiful objects—objects even more useful and beautiful to us than those that are mass-produced and offered for sale by the hundreds.

The work of carving fits into modern life as well as its products. The small work space needed will not take up much precious "house room." Work can be picked up and laid aside at will and it isn't messy. At least no true enthusiast will consider a few chips and shav-

ings a mess! Wood carving has the further advantage of being one of the least expensive of hobbies. Indeed, you can begin with a box end and one tool if you must. It is unlikely that you will ever need more than a dozen tools, although you may indulge yourself to the extent of a few more.

Of all the advantages of wood carving as a hobby, the greatest is this—the special joy that is to be experienced only when hand and brain are partners in the creation of a thing of use and beauty.

13

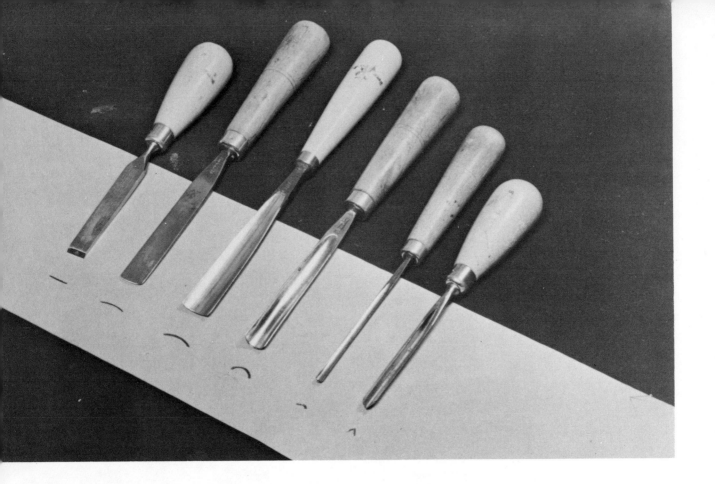

Tools, Accessories and Their Care

CUTTING TOOLS

The cutting tools used for carving wood are gouges and chisels. Chisels have flat blades and make a straight stabbing cut. Gouges have curved blades and consequently make curved stabbing cuts. The exception is the acute-angled V-gouge, sometimes called a V-chisel or veiner. You will recognize this tool of many names on the extreme right in the photographed group of tools on this page. At the extreme left is the straight-bladed chisel. Between these are four curved gouges. Beneath each tool is the stabbing cut it makes.

If you are a beginner, choose such a half-dozen tools from the dozens of shapes and sizes available. The limited number will allow you to become quickly acquainted with the full possibilities and scope of each. Further, if you wait until you feel the need for a specific tool before adding it to your collection you will buy only those immediately useful to you. Made-up sets of tools are often undesirable because they contain little-needed tools. Particularly poor are the very small, stubby-handled gouges sold in sets. These usually lead to small, niggling work in inexperienced hands. Broad, decisive cuts will come easiest with large tools. It is best, therefore, to choose your own collection from those tools which have shanks from four to six inches long and with an overall length including handle from seven to ten inches. Handles may be round or octagonal but should be smooth and feel good in the hand.

If you plan to do chip carving or whittling, add a good knife or two to your tool collection. You will find knives designed especially for these carving crafts.

14

Wood carving tools may be purchased at hardware stores, hobby and craft supply stores and from mail-order establishments specializing in these supplies. Many of the latter will mail tool catalogues on request.

ACCESSORIES

A mallet might be called a tool or an accessory. However classified, it should be round and made of hardwood. Round, because this shape minimizes the chance of striking a glancing blow; hardwood for weight and long wear. It should weigh at least a pound, more for very heavy work. The mallet in the photographed group of accessories is maple.

The whisk broom and pair of C-clamps are hand-protection items. Use the brush to clear the work of chips, not your hands, or you risk splinters. Use the clamps to secure the work to the bench instead of trying to steady it with one hand, or you risk cuts. You need two clamps, for the wood will twist or loosen if only one is used.

The remaining items in the accessory picture are needed for the important task of tool sharpening. The India oilstone has a concave, a convex and a small flat surface, thus accommodating blade contours of most gouges (its use is described on page 17). The flat boxed stone and the small tapered slip stone are both hard Arkansas stone. Not shown, but useful for final stropping of sharpened tools, is a strip of belting leather.

THE WORKBENCH

If work periods are short, a stout kitchen table or an old oak library table will serve as a workbench. It will prove tiring to bend over a low table for long sessions, however, so raise the table by setting it on blocks or acquire a bench of the proper height. Ideally, the work surface should be level with the top of the hip bone as you stand beside it. With a bench of this height, a tall stool is needed for those times when the work permits your being seated. It

is possible to put an old flush door atop stacked concrete building blocks to make a bench, or, lacking a door, a pair of short planks cleated together on the under side. A plan for a bench designed particularly for wood carving is shown at the end of this book.

WOODWORKING TOOLS

Carpenters' woodworking tools do not enter into actual carving processes at all. They are mentioned here because they are so extremely useful in preparing panels, blank shapes and other pieces for carving. For instance, a compass saw or a coping saw will cut the waste away around the outline of a spoon much faster than it can be whittled away. This tool will cut around curved outlines. For sawing along straight lines, carpenters' cross-cut and rip saws are needed. A smooth plane is useful for planing surfaces in preparation for carving and a coarse half-round file will smooth cut edges. With these few tools you can complete many of the projects in this book. Obviously, furniture building and cabinet making will require appropriate tools as well as some knowledge of joinery.

SHARPENING TOOLS

Very sharp tools are the first requirement for successful carving. Even new tools must be sharpened before they can be used and all cut-

Mallet, clamps and sharpening stones are essential accessories for the wood carver.

ting tools require sharpening and resharpening as they are used. To form good habits in this technique, keep sharpening stones, an oil can holding light machine or neat's-foot oil, and a leather strop on the workbench.

Sharpening operations should begin with the fixing of the stone on the bench so it will not slide about. Do this by tacking strips of wood around it or by sinking it into a wooden block or the bench top itself. If tools are new or very dull, the first sharpening is done on the coarse face of a combination fine-coarse carborundum stone. For touching up edges during work, use a hard Arkansas.

After squirting a few drops of oil on the stone, take the handle of your largest and flattest gouge in your right hand and place the convex bevel of the blade so it lies flat on the stone. Note the angle the handle takes when bevel is in this position. Then, with the forefinger of the left hand steadying the blade, and handle angle maintained as it rests along the right wrist, slide the edge from side to side with a firm, even pressure. Roll it just enough to take in the entire curve. Do this four or five times in succession until you feel a slight burr on the inside or concave surface of the blade. If you fail in achieving this burr or roughness, you may be holding the tool at too slight an angle and merely flattening the bevel. Turn the tool over and look at it. Properly sharpened, it will present a smooth surface. If you have exerted more pressure at one point than another, this will be seen as an angle rubbed in the bevel.

When the bevel is smooth and a slight burr raised, the next step is to take the tool in the left hand, concave side up. With the right hand, push the rounded edge of the small slip stone from side to side across blade until burr is gone. Some carvers insist that this rubbing be very light so that no bevel is formed, while others maintain that a very slight bevel on the inside is an advantage. A little experimenting will show which method will give your tools the best "appetite" in use. If a slight bevel is

formed, however, a burr will be raised on the back of the tool, and this, in turn, must be removed in the same manner as the original sharpening but on the hard Arkansas or other finishing stone.

If the first whetting is done on the carborundum, a honing should follow on the hard Arkansas. All oil is then wiped from the tool and it is given a light stropping by placing the convex bevel flat on a strip of leather tacked to the bench and drawing it towards you. Fine emery powder may be dusted on the leather. A small piece of leather may be bent over the forefinger and used to strop inner bevels. In use, tools should get an occasional stropping between touching up or complete sharpenings.

To sharpen the straight-bladed chisels with a bevel on but one side, place bevel flat on stone, and carefully maintaining the original angle of the bevel, draw it backward and forward. Remove the burr very carefully to prevent the forming of a bevel on the non-beveled side. Strop both sides, however, by drawing them along the leather.

Knives are sharpened by pushing and drawing the blade edge over the stone with a circular motion. Rub one side of the blade and then the other, testing for burr with the finger. Strop by drawing it over the leather.

Need for attention, of kind and degree, is determined by the way the tool cuts. The experienced carver doesn't wait for a tool to become obviously dull but automatically hones and strops as he picks up a new tool or pauses to contemplate the next step in the work. The beginner may test for sharpness, both after sharpening a tool or during the work, by cutting across the grain of soft pine. Because pine is so soft, any but the sharpest tools will bruise the fibres rather than slicing them.

In general, it is the very soft and the very hard woods which accent the need for extreme sharpness. It should also be noted that soft wood calls for a long bevel of a less acute angle than the short, steep bevel needed for hard wood. The best bevel for each type of wood can be determined only from much experience. If you find that a particular tool cuts better than others even though they are all sharp, examine the bevel and sharpen the others to conform. In beginning practice it is preferable to strive only to maintain the original bevel of the tool.

GENERAL CARE

The tempered steel of your tools is brittle. It may break or become nicked if the tool is dropped or if edges are allowed to clash. A small nick may be sharpened out on the carborundum but a deep one or a broken corner will make the re-grinding of the tool necessary. You should not attempt grinding your own tools until you are completely acquainted with them in use, until you have seen it done by an expert, and have proper equipment for tool grinding. Happily, barring avoidable accidents, a carving tool, properly sharpened and honed, will serve a long time before re-grinding is called for.

To avoid damaging accidents, carry tools in leather or canvas rolls, a box made purposely for them, or, if they are to be left at the bench, make a rack to put them in between work periods. If they are to be stored, rub each with an oily rag or give them a light waxing.

CARE OF STONES

Stones, too, are brittle and will break if dropped on a hard surface. Make boxes for the larger ones, leather pockets for the slips. Wash them occasionally in warm soap suds, wipe dry and then give them a brief soaking in light machine oil, wiping off any excess.

Flatter gouges are held as shown and slid from side to side with slight roll. A combination fine-coarse carborundum stone is used for first sharpening, a hard Arkansas for final honing.

17

Gouges of extreme curve are held at bevel angle, slid from side to side with rolling motion. Avoid too great a roll, which will round corners— necessitate re-grinding.

Rounded edge of tapered slip stone rubbed gently across inside curve of tool edge sharpens concave side. Test both front and back of cutting edge for "burr" with careful fingertip touch.

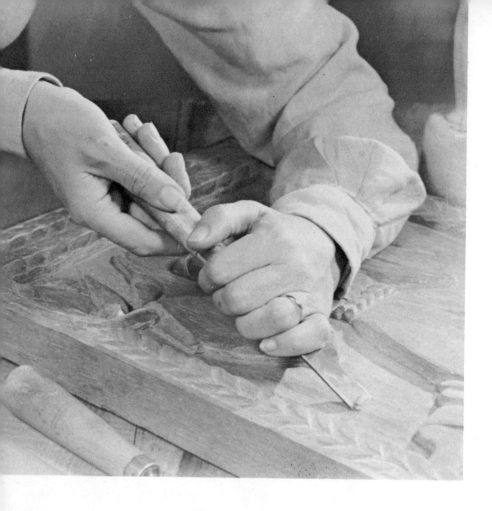

Both hands are on tool,
one pushing, the other guiding
cutting edge, when not using
mallet.

Basic Carving Techniques

BASIC CUTS

Since all types of wood carving utilize certain techniques in common, let us begin with these. Suggestions for practice will follow in the next chapter. Specific details regarding each type of carving will be found in later chapters. It will be seen that however these types of carving vary in finished effect, they are all done with the same basic tool cuts.

The first of these is the "stop-cut." This is a vertical cut which stabs through the wood fibres. The second cut is the "slicing-cut" and it slants downwards at an angle to meet the bottom of the stop-cut and thus remove a chip. (Diag. 1.) Whether done with an axe as in felling a tree or with a wood chisel, the principle of removing wood chips is the same— the stop-cut is made straight into the wood and the slice slants to meet it. The slice should be a smooth cut made in the direction of the grain or across it. (Diags. A, B, C.)

The terms "with the grain," "along the grain" and "across the grain" often puzzle beginners, although such terms are familiar in all fields of woodworking. A glance at a board will show that fibre lines run lengthwise along it and that a cut made along these fibre lines would be "along" the grain while one made at right angles across the board would be "across" the grain. It is not so easy to determine the direction of the grain, and thus cut "with" the grain, by merely looking at it. This is easily discovered, however, by making an experimental cut. When the tool blade is cutting

18

DIAGRAM 1

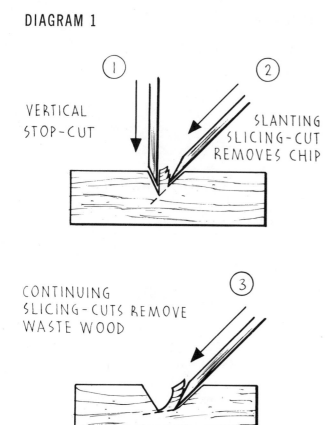

① VERTICAL STOP-CUT

② SLANTING SLICING-CUT REMOVES CHIP

③ CONTINUING SLICING-CUTS REMOVE WASTE WOOD

"with" the grain, a chip or shaving will curl away from the tool, leaving a smooth cut, while the tool itself will seem to rise of its own accord to the surface. If the cut has been started "against" the grain the tool blade will tend to dive and the chip will split or break out roughly. To smooth the cut it will be necessary to turn the work or cut from the other side to make a cut with the grain. (Diag. 2.)

Cutting across the grain, or diagonally across it, is a quick method of clearing waste wood from centers of bowls or from background sections in relief carvings. The rough surface may be finished later by cutting thin slices with the grain to smooth it. Removal of large amounts of wood is usually best done with a large curved gouge, making rough U-shaped troughs or grooves.

Placing of stop-cuts depends on the type of carving being done. If surface decoration is formed with incised troughs or grooves in the wood, stop-cuts will ordinarily follow a center line in groove or trough with the slice starting at a penciled guide line on either side of it and

When driven with mallet, tool must be both held and guided with one hand.

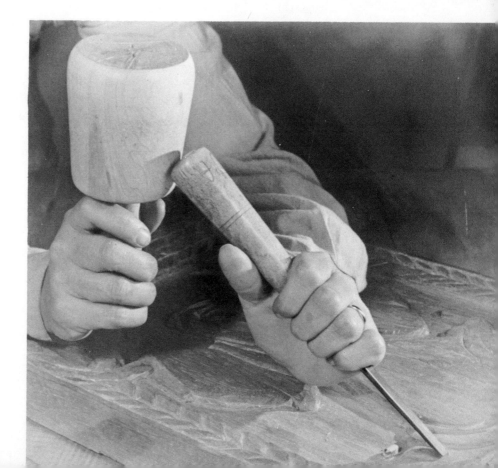

19

sloping downwards to the bottom of the stop-cut. (Diags. A, B, C.) Grooves with rounded bottoms, petals formed by gouging depressions in the wood surface, etc., are made with curved gouges only and do not call for a stop-cut.

A carving in relief, such as the panel used for the photographic illustrations of cuts in this chapter, calls for stop-cuts outlining all motifs or sections of the pattern to be left standing after background waste is removed around it. (Diags. D, E)

For purposes of illustration, let us suppose that you are about to begin the work of cutting such a panel. To begin, choose a tool with edge of approximately the same curve as a part of the outline. Hold it upright by the metal shank in one hand with the edge just slightly outside the penciled guide line. If wood is hard, use mallet to strike end of handle. If soft, a push straight down will do. Drive or push just hard enough to sink blade well into the wood.

It is often desirable to allow the handle of the tool to tilt slightly towards the motif, rather than holding it in a true vertical line, particularly along narrow sections such as borders and stems. Tilting the tool to make the cut slant out will give these delicate parts a slightly wider and stronger base. Avoid under-cutting, which leaves overhanging edges which may break away. (Diag. III.) Speed the work of stabbing the outline by making all the cuts you can with the tool in hand before choosing another and going on with other parts of the outline.

When parts of the design to be left standing are outlined with stop-cuts, make slicing cuts

DIAGRAM 2

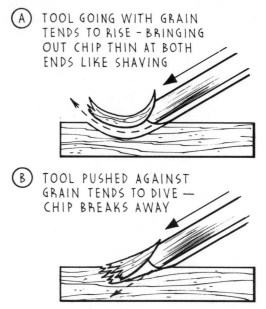

(A) TOOL GOING WITH GRAIN TENDS TO RISE – BRINGING OUT CHIP THIN AT BOTH ENDS LIKE SHAVING

(B) TOOL PUSHED AGAINST GRAIN TENDS TO DIVE – CHIP BREAKS AWAY

in the waste of the background down to the bottom of the vertical cut. If background proves too shallow, repeat stop-cuts. Remove background wood by cutting across or diagonally across grain with as large a gouge as space will permit. Over-all background depth will depend on the thickness of the wood, the type of carving and effect desired and, in some cases, to the use to which the carved piece is put. The background depth need not be strictly uniform over-all—instead, it will look best if slightly deeper in the narrow spaces than in the broader areas.

Modeling of the standing parts of the design is begun when background is roughed out but not yet smoothed. Rough in the various levels with curved gouges. If lowering of certain parts obliterates pencil lines, they may be redrawn or scored with the V-gouge. Work all

DIAGRAM A

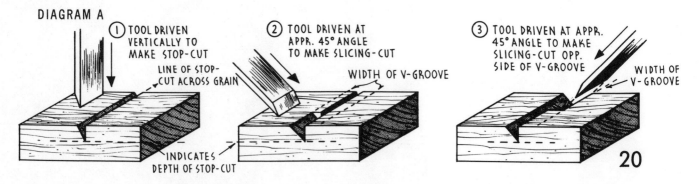

(1) TOOL DRIVEN VERTICALLY TO MAKE STOP-CUT
LINE OF STOP-CUT ACROSS GRAIN
INDICATES DEPTH OF STOP-CUT

(2) TOOL DRIVEN AT APPR. 45° ANGLE TO MAKE SLICING-CUT
WIDTH OF V-GROOVE

(3) TOOL DRIVEN AT APPR. 45° ANGLE TO MAKE SLICING-CUT OPP. SIDE OF V-GROOVE
WIDTH OF V-GROOVE

20

Make "stop-cuts" by matching tool-edge curve to design outline as closely as possible.

Slice wood from background spaces with curved gouges at start, finish by smoothing areas with flatter gouges or chisels.

Tool is often used bevel side up in "modeling" or shaping of rounded parts of raised designs.

DIAGRAM 3

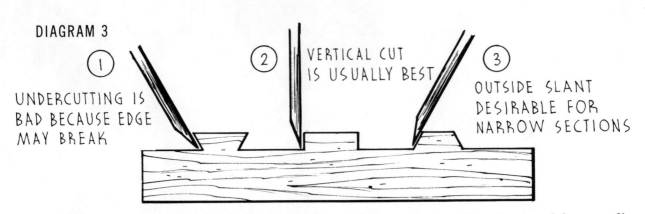

① UNDERCUTTING IS BAD BECAUSE EDGE MAY BREAK

② VERTICAL CUT IS USUALLY BEST

③ OUTSIDE SLANT DESIRABLE FOR NARROW SECTIONS

over the panel at this stage, not finishing any particular section until all roughing-in is complete.

As work progresses on a carving, stand it up or otherwise place it where it will be seen as a finished piece to get the effect of the modeling.

With levels decided upon and rough modeling done, the next step is that of smoothing all surfaces and edges. Use the flatter gouges for this, taking light slicing cuts with the grain. To trim curves and edges these flat gouges are often used bevel side up. Straps, stems and ribbons may have their sharp vertical edges only very slightly rounded while other parts

of the design will be improved by rounding edges gradually to the level of the background. Sharpen lines and borders with light cuts with the V-gouge. If a tool fails to make a bright shiny cut, stop and strop or whet it. Wood fibres should be cut clean, neither torn nor mashed.

In hard wood it will be necessary to use the mallet for most cuts. If you are right-handed, you will hold the mallet in the right hand as you guide and hold the tool in your left hand. Grasp the tool lightly around the shank, driving it with the mallet as you keep your eyes on the blade. The greatest control over the tool

DIAGRAM B

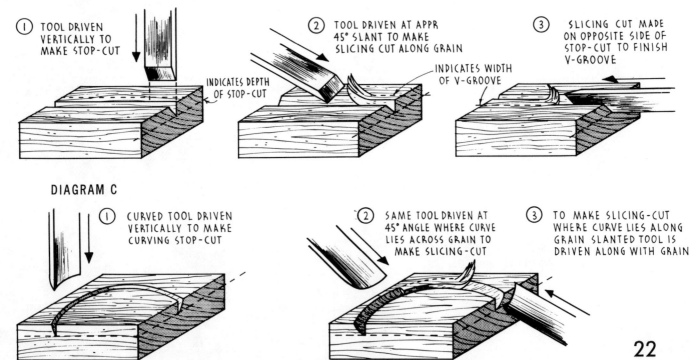

① TOOL DRIVEN VERTICALLY TO MAKE STOP-CUT

INDICATES DEPTH OF STOP-CUT

② TOOL DRIVEN AT APPR 45° SLANT TO MAKE SLICING CUT ALONG GRAIN

INDICATES WIDTH OF V-GROOVE

③ SLICING CUT MADE ON OPPOSITE SIDE OF STOP-CUT TO FINISH V-GROOVE

DIAGRAM C

① CURVED TOOL DRIVEN VERTICALLY TO MAKE CURVING STOP-CUT

② SAME TOOL DRIVEN AT 45° ANGLE WHERE CURVE LIES ACROSS GRAIN TO MAKE SLICING-CUT

③ TO MAKE SLICING-CUT WHERE CURVE LIES ALONG GRAIN SLANTED TOOL IS DRIVEN ALONG WITH GRAIN

22

is to be had in this way and it is a good, basic technique for the beginner to master. There is some temptation to use the mallet to drive a dull tool, but this practice leads to fuzzy edges.

Both hands should be on the tool at all times when not using a mallet. The left hand grasps the tool shank and guides the blade (again, providing you are right-handed), while the right hand drives it by pushing the handle. You will soon notice that the left hand also acts as a brake on the tool, holding it back even as it is being pushed forward with the right hand.

SAFETY RULES

While carving is not unduly hazardous, it does involve edged tools and hence permits the possibility of cuts and scratches if they are improperly handled.

The first safety rule is to keep your hands behind the cutting edge of the tool. Since most types of carving call for both hands on the tool for effective work, this automatically keeps fingers on the safe side. Whittling is the main exception to this, and it is in this type of carv-

ing that the most care must be taken since it is often necessary to cut towards the hand holding the work.

Flat work should be clamped to the bench or held in place within cleats tacked to the bench.

Do not attempt to hold the work down with one hand as you push a tool with the other or you may push it into the flesh of the holding hand! Neither is it a good idea to cut toward the body.

Take care during sharpening and stropping operations to keep your fingers away from the cutting edge.

BREAKAGE

Less serious than cutting yourself, but disappointing nevertheless, is accidental breakage of the work. A slip of the tool may remove a section of the work intended to be left standing in relief, a part of the wood of the background in an incised carving. An over-hearty stroke on the mallet might break off a whole part of a carving in the round. Any of these mishaps will leave a beginner with the feeling that all is lost. Happily, such is not the case,

DIAGRAM D

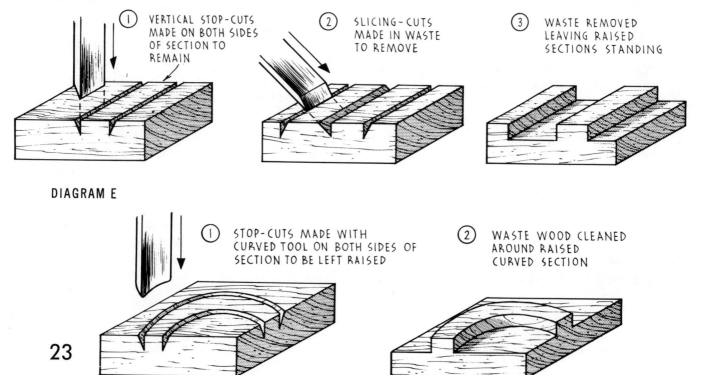

① VERTICAL STOP-CUTS MADE ON BOTH SIDES OF SECTION TO REMAIN

② SLICING-CUTS MADE IN WASTE TO REMOVE

③ WASTE REMOVED LEAVING RAISED SECTIONS STANDING

DIAGRAM E

① STOP-CUTS MADE WITH CURVED TOOL ON BOTH SIDES OF SECTION TO BE LEFT RAISED

② WASTE WOOD CLEANED AROUND RAISED CURVED SECTION

23

for most wood fractures can be easily mended with glue and the repair is rarely noticeable in the finished work.

The powdered resin or casein glues are the most convenient to keep on hand, for they will not be found spilled or dried up just when you need them. You can mix as much or as little of the powdered glue with water as you need. If you use small paper cups and a sliver of wood there will be no brush or container to clean.

Parts are best glued under pressure of clamps or sandbags where it isn't possible to place clamps. Sandbags are easily made by sewing up small bags of closely woven material such as pillow ticking and filling them with sand. Should a large part break in a carving done in the round or a panel split, drill the parts and insert short dowel pins in them to make a stronger join than one using glue alone.

Cracks which open during the course of carving a large work in the round should be ignored for a time. The cracks may close again as surfaces freshly exposed to air become accustomed to the atmosphere. If it does prove necessary to fill them, use beeswax rather than a rigid substance. Other holes and gaps may be filled with plastic wood or with a mixture of sawdust and glue.

PREPARING WOOD FOR CARVING

Wood to be carved is usually purchased as "finished" or, in the parlance of the lumber yard, "S4S," meaning that it has been planed smooth on all four sides, edges considered as sides. In any event, the surface to be carved should be smooth and level, planed either at the mill or by hand with the smooth plane. This is more important if the carving is to form a surface decoration than it is in a work in the round. Whatever the type of carving, wood should not be sanded before carving, because the grit left in the wood fibres will dull tools very rapidly.

Cabinet or carpentry work of cutting out sections or parts, the sawing of construction joints such as mortises or dovetails, should be done before carving. Assembly and over-all application of wood finishes should be done after carving is complete. This is the most desirable plan of work in the making of a chest or other furniture, for it permits planning the carving patterns to fit exact spaces and it prevents damage to the carving that might result from cutting the construction joints afterward.

In laying out designs it is usually better to plan for borders of plain wood around carved sections rather than to bring the carving to the very edge of the wood. Such margins are particularly desirable over half-lap edges and similar construction cuts.

TRANSFERRING DESIGNS TO WOOD

When wood surfaces are smooth and parts or sections cut to size, the next step in preparing to carve is the transferring of the design to the wood. If the design is a simple geometric pattern previously planned for the space, the drawing may be done directly on the wood with pencil, ruler and drawing compass. More complicated patterns are drawn to size on paper first and then traced on the wood with carbon paper. Fasten drawings and carbon in place with thumb tacks or drafting tape. If using tacks, place them in a portion of the design which will be cut away as background to avoid leaving pinholes in your work.

Cut-outs, as described in the chapter on designs for carving, may be held in place with tape and drawn around. Whatever the type of design or the means used to transfer it, use a hard, sharp pencil and enough pressure to make a firm line heavy enough to be clearly followed with the cutting tools. Careful and accurate drawings will add to the pleasure of carving.

A first step is becoming acquainted with tools. Make practice cuts to explore the full possibilities of each one you own.

Suggestions for Practice

MAKING A GOOD START

Much of your pleasure in wood carving will depend on how you start. While it is a maxim that all beginnings are hard, this section is planned to help you make a beginning that is easy. After all, an occupation taken up for pleasure must give pleasure or be abandoned! The value of any hobby is destroyed when it brings frustration instead of fun. You owe it to yourself, then, to make an intelligent beginning.

To avoid initial disappointment, first get acquainted with your tools by making a few experiments with them. In the course of these you will learn something of the way wood behaves when cut with the different tools. Don't be discouraged about tool sharpening. You will learn to do this as you go along with the other phases of carving. Above all, ignore any

suggestion to the effect that you start with pine, because this soft wood requires the very sharpest tools! Pine is a pleasant carving wood, but not when it is used by a beginner whose tools may be less than sharp.

Philippine mahogany, an inexpensive hardwood which is neither hard nor soft, is good material for a practice board. So is clear redwood.

The practice board shown in this chapter is of Philippine mahogany and was cut with the two tools shown with it. The few grooves at the bottom were cut with the V-gouge, a somewhat specialized tool used mostly for cleaning up and sharpening outlines. Since all the other cuts on the board were made with the large curved gouge used alone, it is easy to see how a tool of this kind can produce many different textures and designs.

Provide yourself with a piece of amenable wood, clamp it to the bench and, choosing one of your larger gouges, make various cuts with it to get as many different effects as you can. Hold the gouge upright and drive it into the wood to make vertical cuts in a row to form a border of half-circles and a few full circles. Rounding off the top of the wood inside the circles will result in what the wood-carver terms a "pearl"; removing the wood below the row of half-circles will make a scalloped border. Troughs and grooves combined with vertical cuts give other effects. Try variations of spacing, both with and across the grain.

If the wood splits or splinters when you make vertical cuts you may be using more force to drive the tool than is necessary. In making the rounded troughs, do not try to make them full depth with one cut; instead go along the trough several times. The tool, if sufficiently sharp, should slide smoothly and easily along the grain, seeming to rise to the surface and thus remove a chip almost of its own accord. You will know you are working against the grain when the blade wants to dig in sharply and chips break off.

CHOOSING A FIRST PROJECT

Because the rudiments of carving are so quickly learned you should now be ready to start a simple project. You may even be tempted to tackle an intricate one, and although you might well succeed with it, in the interests of self-encouragement you will do well to start in a smaller way. A decorated bread board, a small mirror frame, a bowl, scoop or box are all good pieces to begin on. Decorate your piece with strap carving, chip carving or an incised design or lettering.

One type of carving is neither easier nor harder to do than another, although some are more time-consuming. The factor which has the most bearing on the matter is the type of wood chosen. A wood that is successful for one type might fail with another. In general, the inex-

perienced carver will have the most success, whatever the type of carving he decides to start with, if he uses a medium-hard or medium-soft wood. More specific information on matching kinds of wood to carving types is given in the chapters describing techniques used for the different kinds of carving and in the chapter on Woods for Carving.

Another factor where the happy medium will serve the beginner is in the size of the motifs to be used. Small work is a disadvantage because it can be picky and frustrating. Larger designs permit the use of larger tools and give room for the sweep of action that best develops good habits and good carving.

HOW TO JUDGE CARVINGS

Without going into the field of aesthetics, it is possible to sort good carvings from bad. You should learn to judge them in order to improve your own work. Since the perfectionist never

Progress in carving a flat raised pattern
shows first pencilled outline (upper right-hand quarter)
stop-cuts, background removed and slight modeling
of finished work (lower right-hand quarter).

Wood scraps and inexpensive wooden bowls and spoons
may be used for the beginner's practice.
Incised V-cuts decorate these useful household items.

has much fun anyhow, refrain from being super-critical of your own work at the start. Then, any carving you do which gives you pleasure may be considered good!

Let no other carvers off so easily, though! Look critically and long at every piece of carving you find in museums, churches, public buildings, art shops. You will notice that some carving looks very crude when you look at it closely. The tool marks may be coarse and there is little apparent finish. If, however, this same carving looks strong and forceful from

a few steps away, it is a good carving. If a surface has been made more interesting by the designs or patterns cut in it, is more pleasant to contemplate because of the resulting play of light upon it, it is good carving. Small carved objects meant to be handled must feel good in the hand. To be called good they must have that intimate charm which comes when grace has been added to usefulness.

27

A carved sundial tells "garden-time" and advises,
"Let no one speak ill of the day till night has come."

How to do Incised Carving

This type of carving is readily recognized by the fact that the designs are made by incisions in the wood, the original surface left untouched as background. Instead of the surface modeling being employed to gain the several levels that make carving in relief effective, the depth of the cuts are varied in incised carving. These cuts may form grooves, troughs with rounded or sharp V-shape bottoms, inverted pyramids such as distinguish chip carving, and many other variously shaped depressions. The simplest of carvings done in this manner may have much appeal for the very reason of its simplicity and lack of pretension.

APPROPRIATE USES

While lending itself to the decoration of many household objects, incised carving is the base for many more. A simple design cut in this way will result in a raised design on butter, cookie or pastry dough. If a member of your family or a friend does leather craft or ceramics he will appreciate leather stamps for embossing damp leather or a potter's mark to press into the unfired clay. Stamps and presses are usually cut from hard wood that will take fine detail without breaking. A further consideration is wearability, although this is not important in pastry presses.

28

Incised carving can be added to many wooden-ware articles to be found in household departments of "variety stores." Wooden spoons, bowls, bread boards and small rolling pins can be made into serving and baking accessories for your home or for your friends.

MATERIALS

Since the danger of breaking off of raised motifs is always present in the work of carving in relief, softwoods are seldom used. They suffer no such disadvantage in incised carving; instead they seem made to order for it. Although any wood may be used for this type of carving, give preference, especially if you are a beginner, to redwood, cedar, or Philippine mahogany. Soft wood and the simple technique make this one of the quickest and easiest ways of getting an effect out of all proportion to the effort put into it.

TECHNIQUE

When the design has been transferred to the prepared wood, the first step is to make depth cuts along the center of all parts to be cut as grooves or V-shaped troughs. Petals and other round-bottomed depressions are scooped out with rounded gouges and will not need depth cuts. You will soon become accustomed to giving the tool a uniform push or drive with the mallet to make depth cuts of an even depth. You will also note that the tool sinks more deeply when the blade follows grain than when it cuts across it and decrease or increase pressure on it accordingly. Match curves of tool blades to curves of the design as closely as possible. Make as many cuts with one tool as you can before picking up another.

With depth cuts made, the next step is to make slanting slicing cuts, using the outer edge of the penciled design as starting guide lines, sloping cut to meet bottom of the depth cut, and release chip. Make as many slicing cuts as needed to make a smooth-sided depression, repeating depth cuts where more depth is de-

29

sired. The V-gouge is indispensable here to sharpen lines and clean up bottom of trough and boat-shaped sections.

You will notice that chips are removed most easily and the cuts of the tool are more effective when the depth cut is across the grain and the slanting cut with it. For this reason, it is best wherever possible to have the main lines of a design go across the grain of your panel.

Circular grooves present a problem in that a part of the circle follows the grain and then curves across it. A little practice will show that best results are obtained when one side of the groove is approached from one angle, the other from another. This usually means turning the work end for end unless you can walk around it, so make as many effective cuts as you can while the work is in one position.

INCISED LETTERING

Clear and dignified lettering, clean-cut and well spaced, can form beautiful and satisfying decoration. This applies to letters either carved in relief or incised, but the latter are by far the easiest to carve. Single initials, monograms, names, dates, suitable quotations or mottoes all find a place in carved decoration.

Classical type faces, rather than brush letters,

"Perpetua", a printing type-face, looks like this when adapted for a carved letter.

 ABCDEFGHIJK
LMNOPQRSTU
VWXYZ·1234567890

Hadriano alphabet, its letter A laid out for carving.
Dotted lines indicate where depth cut is made.

are better suited to carving. Good examples are shown in this chapter.

When the letter to be carved is chosen, care must be taken to retain its characteristics. Falsified proportions or any distortion of line will cause letters to lose identity. Whole words or sentences should never be made up entirely of capitals when a "text" letter is used, such as the German or Goudy Text shown here. Because they were designed to do so, Roman letters, of which Hadriano is an example, may form words and sentences entirely made up of capital letters. There were no lower-case letters in the original Roman alphabet—only capitals.

One of the easiest ways to copy and enlarge letters for carving is to make inked tracings or actual photographs of the letters and "blow them up" in a photographic enlarger. From the enlarger, the image is projected onto drawing paper and outline drawn. They may also be copied by tracing the originals onto paper lined in squares and then drawing them free-hand over larger squares.

Spacing and alignment are important. Spacing is not difficult if letters are viewed in relation to their companions and the space around them, rather than the space between the letter

bases. Letters are seldom spaced an equal distance apart along a bottom line. Also, the letter bases do not rest on a common line. If in doubt about spacing or alignment, pin up a drawing of your proposed lettering and observe it for a few days. A mistake will jump out, if not the first time you look at it, the tenth or eleventh.

After layout is approved and transferred to the wood (so that letters run across the grain, lettering running lengthwise of the board) center lines are drawn on each stroke of each letter to mark the position of the depth cut. This cut is made as previously described, depth depending on size of the letter, thickness of the wood, and the degree of boldness wanted. Usually the deepest part is in the main strokes of the letter, becoming shallower at cross strokes, flourishes, and serifs ("tails" at the end of strokes). Slice towards this cut from each side. Serifs are treated as in chip carving, by making a stabbed cut in each angle and slicing out small chips.

The carving of letters will go with speed if all vertical depth cuts are made down the center of main strokes of letters, right-hand slopes all cut and the work then turned and left-hand slopes made. Finish curves and fine strokes last.

30

Following the pencilled outlines, stop cut is made along the center of each stroke with tool that matches curvature of center line.

With gouge curved to correspond with letter, slanted cut is made next, to meet bottom of stop cut. On convex curves, use gouge bevel side up.

V-gouge finishes carving by cleaning, sharpening bottom of trough and cutting narrow cross strokes, flourishes, and serifs.

This sign is finished with a light stain, letters left darker than the surface for accent. Lettering used is Lichte Weiss Fractur, a German type face.

31

ABCDEFG
HIJKLMN
OPQRSTUVW
XYZ · 1234567890
abcdefghijklmnop
qrstuvwxyz

Lichte Weiss-Fractur, a German type face

ABCDEFGHIJKLMN
OPQRSTUVWXYZ
abcdefghijklmnopqrstuvwxyz

Goudy Text

ABCDEF

GHIJKL

MNOPQR

STUVWX

YZ & 123

4567890

Perpetua Title

33

ABCDEFG

HIJKLMN

OPQRSTU

VWXYZ &

1234567890

Lydian

34

ABCDEFGH
IJKLMNO
PQRSTUVW
XYZ & abcdefghij
klmnopqrstuvwxyz
1 2 3 4 5 6 7 8 9 0

Legend

35

PROJECT NO. 1 • Knife Holder

All you need are scraps of white pine or other soft wood and ½-inch doweling to make this knife holder.

Carving is done after pieces are cut to shape, holes drilled and knife slots cut, but before assembly. Carving must be shallow to avoid cutting through to knife slots.

Cut curved lines of the back piece on a band saw or by hand with a coping saw. Cut slots for knives in the back of the face piece to the depths shown on the drawing. Drill holes for the dowel pins through the back piece and to within ¼ inch of the front surface of the face piece.

Assemble by inserting dowel pins in holes. Glue will hold them secure. Lengthen dowel pins if wide-bladed knives are to be accommodated in this holder.

Give antique finish by applying a mixture of burnt umber oil color and boiled linseed oil, and by rubbing in wax when oil has dried. For natural finish, sand and shellac.

PROJECT NO. 2 • Cup Shelves

These hanging shelves will display individual cups and saucers from your collection, or hold small trailing house plants.

Those pictured here were made of Philippine mahogany, finished with clear shellac and paste wax. Pine would be attractive too, particularly if given an antique finish.

Cut the pieces as shown on the pattern from stock ⅜ inch thick. Note the groove in which the saucer stands. Make deep enough to hold the saucer rim securely.

Carve design on back and the curved grooves on shelf front before assembling the parts. Assemble with glue and small brads in this order: join the sides to the back, slip the bottom between the sides and against the back, and put on the front strip. Round all edges after assembly. Sand all surfaces thoroughly before applying finish.

This shelf was designed for "small blacks." If your cups are larger, proportions of the shelf may be changed.

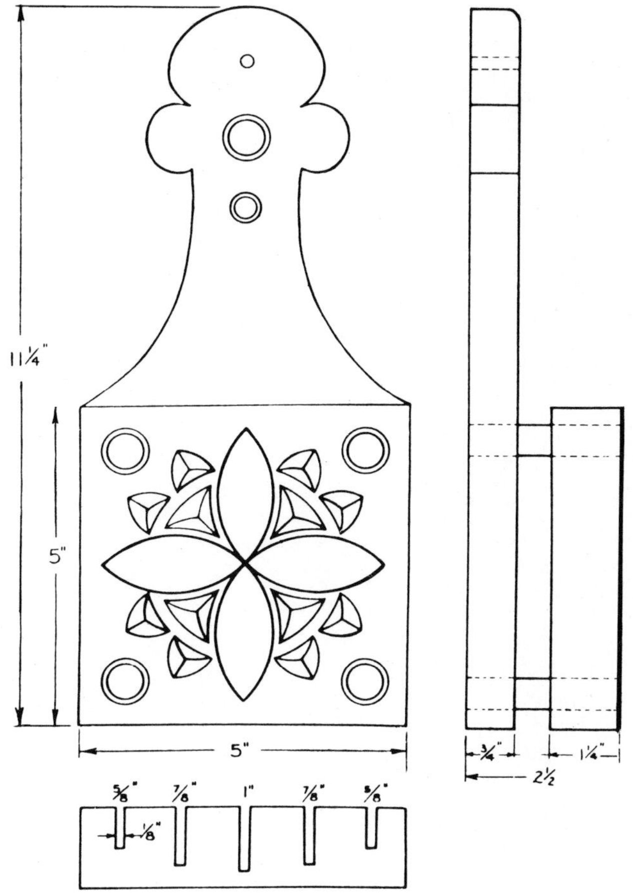
11¼"
5"
5"
¾"
1¼"
2½"
5/8"
7/8"
1"
7/8"
5/8"
1/8"

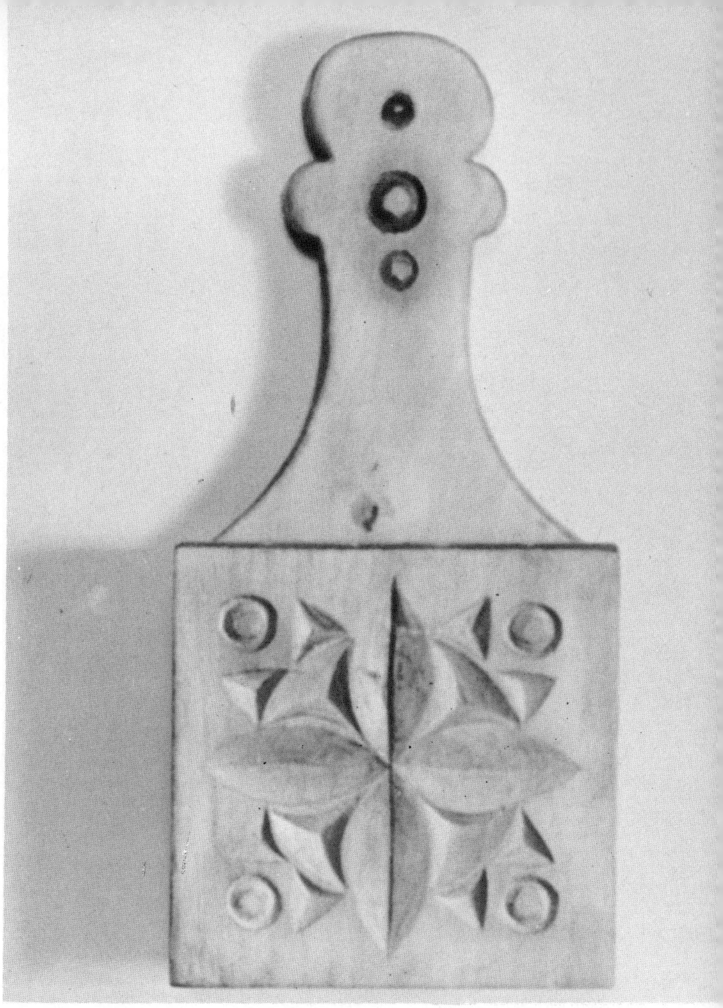

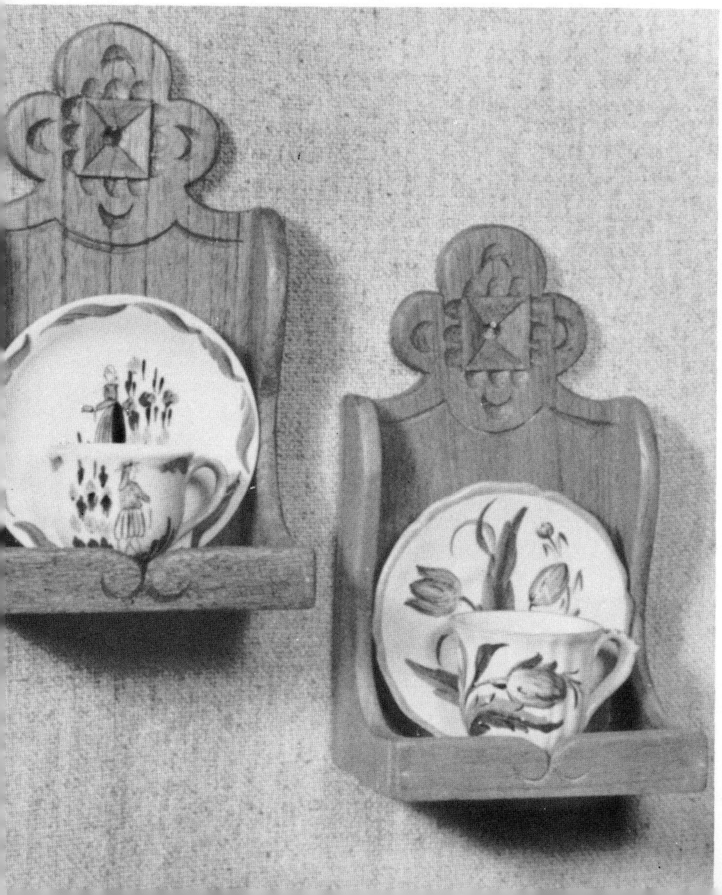

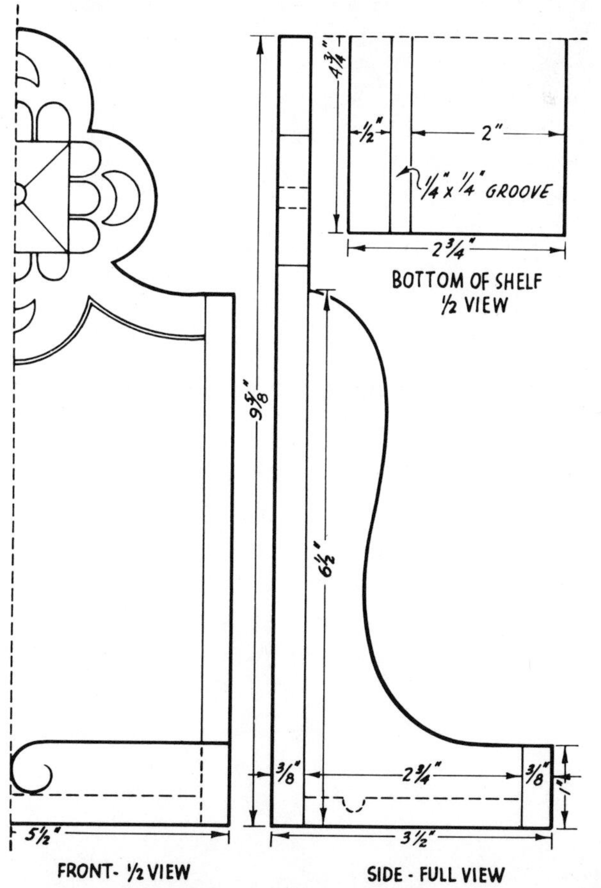
4¾"
½"
2"
¼" x ¼" GROOVE
2¾"
BOTTOM OF SHELF
½ VIEW
9⅞"
6½"
⅜"
2¾"
⅜"
1"
5½"
3½"
FRONT- ½ VIEW
SIDE - FULL VIEW

Italian hearthside accessory
adapts to outdoor use.

PROJECT NO. 3 • Dustpan Flower Shelf

This Italian dustpan makes a decorative garden shelf for displaying potted plants.

Cut pieces as shown in the drawing and carve outline cuts before assembling. Stock for handle is 1 inch thick; all other parts ½ inch thick. Carve the side pieces inside and out,

and round the upper and front edges. Join back and sides with dovetail joints for strength. Attach the bottom with small finishing nails. Use waterproof glue for all joints to withstand exposure to weather.

A scalloped copper strip faces and protects the

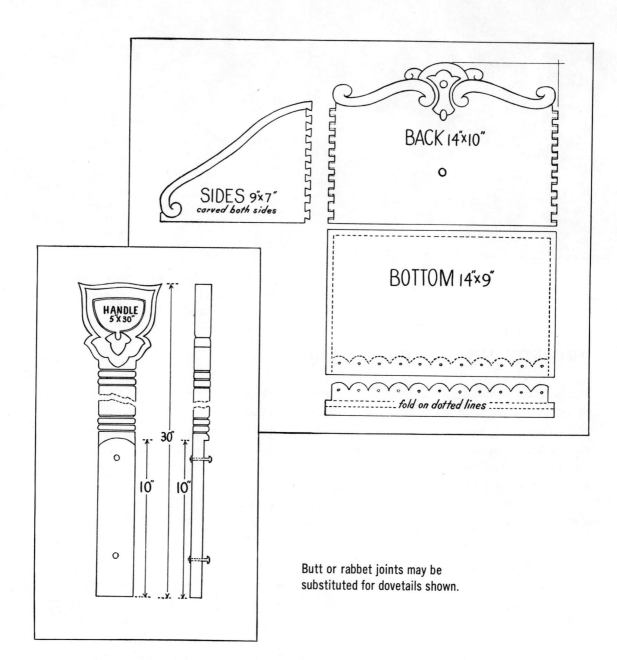

SIDES 9"x7"
carved both sides

BACK 14"x10"

BOTTOM 14"x9"

HANDLE 5"x30"

30"

10"   10"

fold on dotted lines

Butt or rabbet joints may be
substituted for dovetails shown.

slightly sloping front edge. Fasten it directly to the wood with copper tacks and then shape to fold underneath.

Fasten the long, carved handle to the box with two black iron carriage bolts. Smooth and round all edges.

The finish, if the wood used is light in color, is a stain made by mixing a small quantity of burnt umber in linseed oil. Rub it into the sur-face of the wood with a soft cloth to clear the grain and give it an antique look. When the stain is thoroughly dry, apply further rub-bings of linseed oil followed with paste wax as a final coat. An antique blue finish can be achieved by mixing very small amounts of Prussian blue and black oil colors in linseed oil, applying the mixture with a soft cloth, and then wiping the wood grain clear.

39

One-pound mold closed and ready for butter
to be pressed into it (left), and open for removal
of butter and washing (at right).

PROJECT NO. 4 • Butter Molds

Molds for applying decorative designs to butter cubes or patties offer an interesting project.

The types shown here—a generous and sturdy two-pound mold; a one-pound mold, hinged to make removal of the molded butter easy; and a smaller mold that decorates individual pats with a five-pointed star—are simply and fairly obviously constructed. The small, round molds are turned on a lathe; the others are easily made with hand tools.

Use any close-grained hardwood. Maple is good, although sometimes difficult to carve. Sandpaper uncarved surfaces to extreme smoothness, and leave the wood natural or give it a highly polished coat of pure beeswax (any oily or turpentine mixtures might taint the butter).

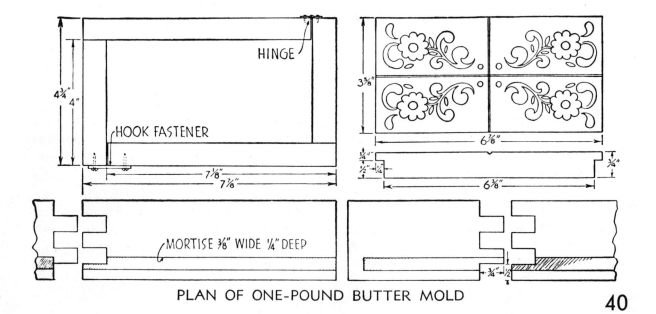

HINGE

HOOK FASTENER

4¾"
4"

7⅞"
7⅞"

MORTISE ⅜" WIDE ¼" DEEP

3⅜"

6⅞"

¼"
½" ¼

6⅜"

¾"

¾" ½

PLAN OF ONE-POUND BUTTER MOLD

40

TWO-POUND BUTTER MOLD

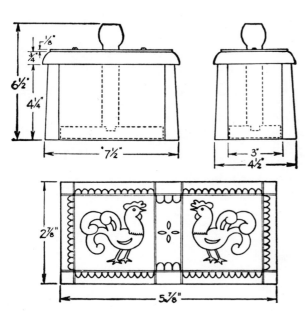

Two-pound mold on its side, stamp block protruding to show detail of intaglio design.

INDIVIDUAL BUTTER MOLD

Bottom view shows the die of mold, which leaves raised star-border pattern on butter.

Side view of lathe-turned mold that forms individual pats. Maple is a good mold wood.

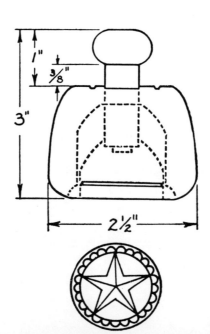

PROJECT NO. 5 • Serving Plank

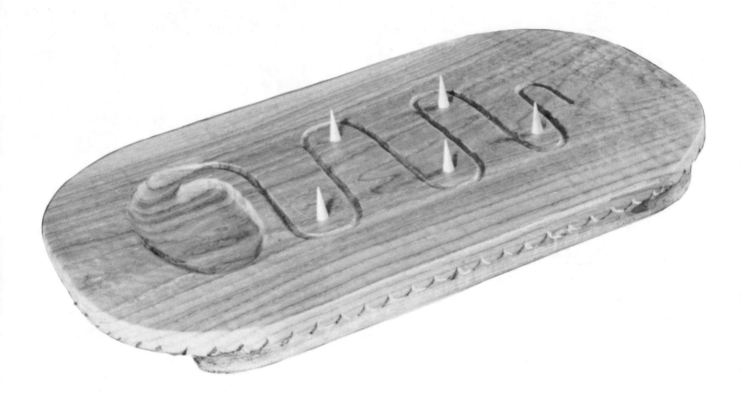

A well-oiled plank has been the platform on which has been built many a reputation for serving good food. Even a hamburger tastes better on such a background, as a hot oak plank holds heat and imparts a subtle flavor of the wood.

To make the plank you will need: 1¼ by 12-inch oak plank 20 inches long; ¼-inch maple dowels, enough to make five pegs 1¼ inches long, and a few extras.

Trace the outline of the finished plank on the oak board. In order that curves at ends will be the same, fold a rectangular piece of paper the size of the board in half lengthwise, and then in half again crosswise. Cut out the curve

of the corners with scissors; unfold, place on plank, and trace.

To cut the handholds, turn the plank upside down and saw to a depth of ⅝ inch, 2 inches in from each end. This is "cut No. 1" in dia-

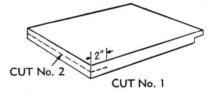

CUT No. 2   2"   CUT No. 1

gram. Make a second cut in from each end at right angles to the first, and remove wood for handholds. This is "cut No. 2" in diagram. Now round off corners with a coping saw.

Next, mark on the board the pattern for the ¼-inch gravy groove and oval-shaped well, which should be about 6 by 3½ inches. Cut groove with small, sharply curved gouge, digging slightly deeper as it approaches the well. With a shallow-curved gouge, carve out the well, sloping the sides toward the center until it is ½ inch deep.

To scallop the border, hold plank firmly on edge (use vise if you have it) and with a mallet drive the larger curved gouge straight down into the wood ⅛ inch. Continue around the plank. Undercut the wood below the scallop with a flat chisel.

Smooth off top of plank with flat gouge and sand lightly with fine sandpaper.

Mark locations for removable pegs about 1 inch in from the curves of the groove, and drill holes for pegs ¼ inch deep. Pegs should fit snugly, but not so tightly that they can't be removed.

To make pegs, point one end of the ¼-inch dowel in a pencil sharpener. Cut off 1¼-inch peg. Continue sharpening and cutting until you have five pegs and spares.

Before using the plank for the first time, coat the surface generously with salad oil and place in a hot oven for a few minutes so that the oil will penetrate the wood. Repeat this process once or twice until the wood has absorbed all possible oil. Wipe off surplus oil before storing in a large paper sack or cloth.

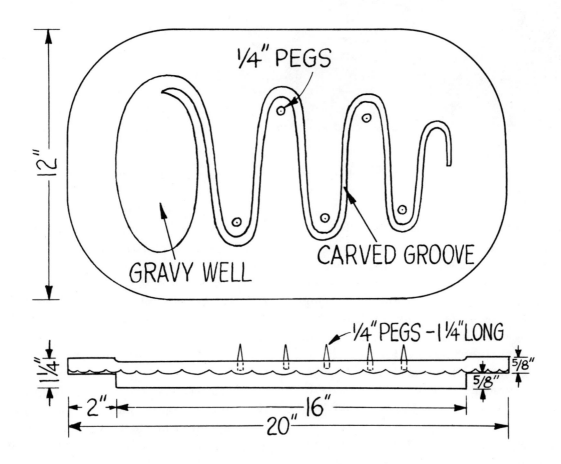

PROJECT NO. 6 • Marriage Chest

Cabinet work on this redwood chest calls for ordinary tools.

The design of this marriage chest was inspired by one carved in Spain in the 17th century. The chest is not difficult to construct. It can be built with ordinary carpenter's tools.

The chest is made of redwood. Clear, straight-grained matched boards should be used to assure good color under the natural shellac-and-wax finish and to provide an easy carving surface. It is formed of boards glued together two boards wide and cut to size. For sides and ends, use 1 by 8-inch boards; for lid and bottom, use 1 by 12's. Feet are cut from 2 by 4's. Proper work sequence is to cut the parts to size, carve the panels, and then assemble the chest.

Glue the boards together and cut them to size. Lay out the dovetails with which the box is joined, and cut them to fit. Trace the carving design directly on the wood and carve it into the surface. The type chosen for the lettering is a copy of an old stone-cut letter, the typeface known as "Hadriano."

The hinged lid and the bottom overhang 1 inch on three sides, the back being flush. Fasten the bottom to the body of the box with glue and screws. Strengthen all joints with glue. Attach the feet with screws through the bottom of the chest, and glue the scalloped apron across the front and over faces of front feet.

Paint the interior of chest in a bright color if you like. The chest shown is thus lined with two coats of bright blue enamel. The painted area is kept inside a scalloped line on inside of lid so the color does not show on the overhanging edge of lid.

You must have a pair of offset hinges for this type of lid. Lid lifts and lock are optional. To make a handmade lock-plate for a purchased lock, cut plate to rough shape from light sheet iron with cold chisel. File to finished outline. Then drill hole to fit lock barrel and small holes for fancy-headed upholstery tacks to hold it in place.

Sand all uncarved parts thoroughly. Apply several coats of clear shellac thinned with alcohol—sand each coat lightly after it is completely dry. Coats of well-rubbed paste wax give added protection to the surface.

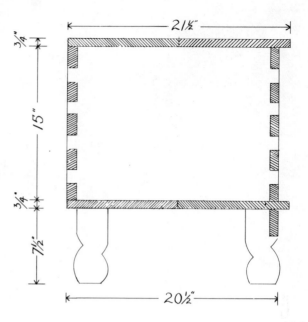

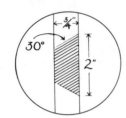

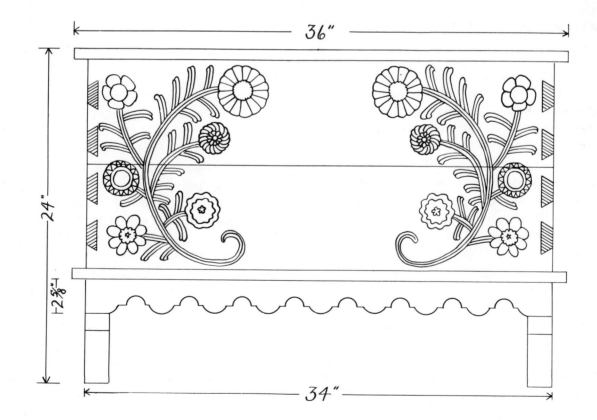

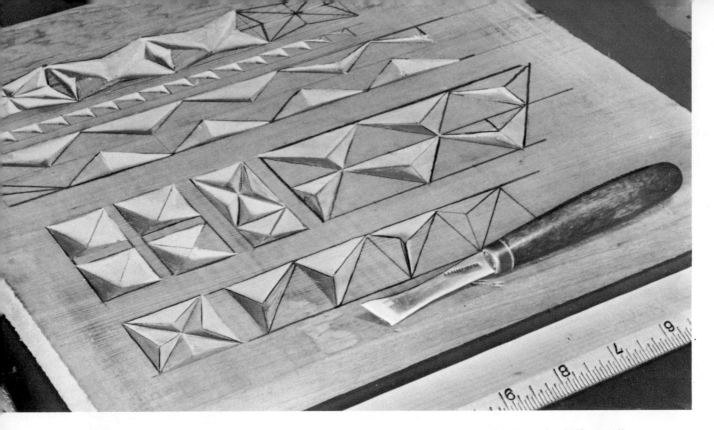

A pencil, ruler and chip carving knife are all you need to plan and carve a "sampler" in soft wood.

How to do Chip Carving

This is a favorite form of carving, particularly with beginners and young people, because of the ease with which maximum decorative results are to be had and because of the minimum tool requirement. Chip carving is often taught as a craft in itself, without reference to other types of carving. It is, however, a kind of incised carving, the incisions grouped to form geometric patterns. The triangle is the base of most chip carving designs and the infinite possibilities of arrangement of these make designing simple and easy.

While chip carving used alone will make a rich and satisfying surface decoration for book covers, border designs on furniture or architectural details, cookie and butter stamps, chests and boxes of all kinds, etc., it also combines well with other types of carving. Consider it when planning any piece which would be enhanced with large sections of surface carving.

MATERIALS

Wood chosen for chip carving should have a straight, even grain without pronounced color striping. Knots or wavy grain will interfere with the easy removal of the straight-sided chips, while strong changes of color will spoil the visual effects of the design. Wood may be soft, such as redwood, pine, or cedar; or medium-hard, such as walnut or mahogany. As much of the charm of this type of carving lies in removing each chip with a single slice of the tool, very hard woods such as maple or butternut are not recommended. Whatever the wood, it should have a smooth, planed but not sanded, surface.

TOOLS

Chip carving done in soft woods calls for but a single tool, a sharp skew-bladed knife. The cedar desk box and the redwood garden box illustrated in this chapter were carved with

Make stop or "stab cuts" deepest at center where lines intersect by holding straight-bladed chisel at angle. Drive with mallet in hard wood.

this knife. The thin blade is, however, too flexible for cutting hard wood. Chip carving done in hard wood will require the use of a rigid chisel, either straight or skew-bladed, and a mallet. A flat sharpening stone is needed to keep the edge keen and clamps are essential to hold the stock firmly in place.

TRANSFERRING DESIGNS

Simple chip carving designs may be drawn directly on the wood with pencil or they may be drawn on paper and transferred to the wood by tracing them over carbon paper. When using more complicated patterns or designs which call for many penciled lines which would not be removed when carving was completed, draw the entire pattern on tissue and attach it to the wood with rubber cement. Cut right through the paper. Rub off remaining bits of paper and cement when cutting is finished.

TECHNIQUE

Begin by ruling several triangles with base lines about 1 inch long on a piece of soft wood. Divide these by drawing a line in from each corner to meet at the center, thus making three small triangles within each large one.

Make stab cuts along the inner lines to sever the wood fibres on two sides of each small triangle. Then make a slanted slicing cut along the outside guide line to remove the entire chip. When the three chips are cut away an inverted pyramid-shaped depression is left.

To make stab cuts with the knife, hold it upright with the tip of the blade placed where lines intersect in the center and blade directly along line. Give it a straight push downward until the heel of the blade touches the outside guide line. This automatically gives a uniform slanting cut with greatest depth at the center.

To make stab cuts with a straight-bladed chisel, tip it so one point of the blade sinks to proper depth at the center.

To remove chip, use the same tool used to make stab cuts. Holding it at an angle, push it to make a slicing cut from the outside guide line to meet the bottom of the stab cut.

Carve with the grain and strive to keep angles of sloping planes uniform. In hard wood, or when removing large chips, it may be necessary to take several slicing cuts to get sufficient depth and to obtain even sides and slopes.

When the basic technique of making the two cutting motions in chip carving is mastered by practice on the simple triangle, it will be obvious that many types of triangles and arrangements of these may be used to form effective chip-carving patterns. Curved lines may be introduced for further variety. Use a curved chisel to remove chips in the same way as the straight-sided ones.

To remove chip, start slanting cut at outside line of triangle and slope cut to bottom of stab cut. Cut with the grain of the wood.

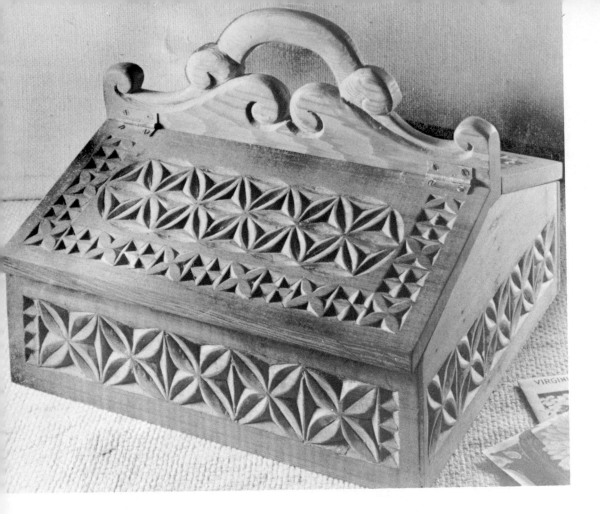

PROJECT NO. 7 • Garden Seed Box

With seed packets in one side and your dibble, favorite trowel, and garden gloves in the other, this divided carryall box of redwood is ready to go "on location" when you garden. It would provide portable storage for many types of small objects should you desire to put it to a different use.

Wood used for center dividing piece with handle is ¾ inch thick; ends, sides, and lids are ½ inch thick. Bottom is ¼-inch plywood. Stock for the parts to be chip carved was chosen for its fine straight grain. This characteristic was avoided, however, in the choice of the piece for the handle lest splitting occur either during carving or later use of the box.

To make this box, begin by cutting out parts to size and shape as shown on drawing. Cut carved lines of handle section with coping saw or band saw. To cut opening for handhold, drill and saw with coping saw or carve waste wood away. Round the edges by carving and filing with wood rasp. Complete chip carving on lids, sides and ends before putting box together.

Join the box with waterproof glue and small brads. Center the dividing middle section across plywood bottom, tacking it in place from the underside, and assemble ends and sides around these. Four small brass hinges will be needed to fasten lid sections to the upright dividing section.

This redwood box may be finished by giving it several coats of the penetrating oil made primarily for preserving redwood, or linseed oil and wax may be used.

48

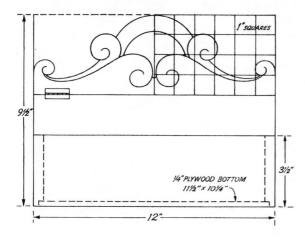

1" SQUARES

9½"

¼" PLYWOOD BOTTOM
11½" x 10¼"

3½"

12"

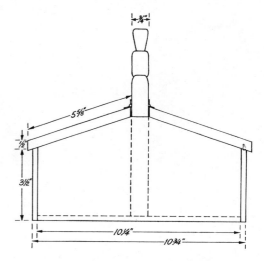

¾"

5⅝"

½"

3½"

10¼"

10¾"

CARVING DESIGN FOR LIDS

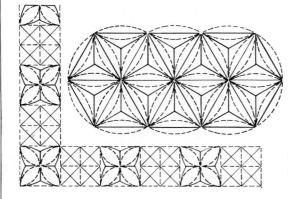

CARVING DESIGN – SIDES–ENDS

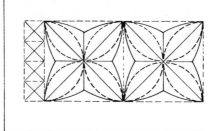

Depth cuts made on solid lines, sloping slicing-cuts
start from dotted lines.

Garden box being assembled with glue
and brads after parts are carved.

Stationery box of cedar decorated with simple chip carving designs and antique brass handle.

PROJECT NO. 8 • Desk Box

Although this box is designed to hold Monarch size stationery, it could serve other purposes equally well. Dividing sections in the interior would adapt it to a desk "organizer" to hold paper clips, rubber bands, stamps and the many other small items that should be kept conveniently in one place.

Soft red cedar is one of the finest woods for chip carving and was chosen as the material for this box. Plane the stock for the free-lifting unhinged lid to ⅝-inch thickness; sides and ends to ½ inch. Bottom is ¼-inch plywood. Study drawing and photograph for construction details, noting that box corners are mor-

tised to make half-lap joints and that plywood bottom fits into rabbet cut in sides and ends. Edges of lid are reduced in thickness; the center is left full thickness.

Lay carving patterns out and carve before assembling box. When carving is completed, assemble box with glue only. Hold with furniture clamps until glue is set.

The decorative handle used on this box is a finely made antique brass drawer pull. Finish box with linseed oil thinned with turpentine after all uncarved portions are thoroughly sanded. Polish finally with furniture wax applied and rubbed with a soft cloth.

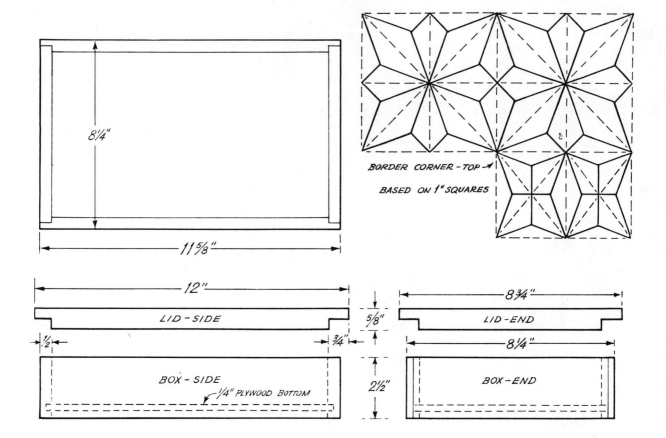

8¼"

11⅝"

BORDER CORNER - TOP →

BASED ON 1" SQUARES

12"

LID - SIDE

5/8"

8¾"

LID - END

½

¾"

8¼"

BOX - SIDE

¼" PLYWOOD BOTTOM

2½"

BOX - END

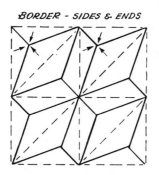

BORDER - SIDES & ENDS

Box being assembled with
glue after parts are carved.
Note end-lap and
rabbet joints.

51

Wayfarer's shrine for the garden has relief carved panel depicting St. Francis.

Carving in Relief

HIGH AND LOW RELIEF

Carving in high or deep relief, and carving in low or shallow relief, are sometimes considered as separate types. They will be considered here as but one since they differ only in degree of depth and elaboration of modeling.

Carving in relief is generally considered the next step after incised or chip carving. Any carving—and it may be merely a flat pattern outlined with chisel cuts and the background wood removed to a depth of about ⅛ inch—in which the motif stands above a sunken background is considered relief carving. In some cases, the carved motifs so fill the design area that there is little or no background, as illustrated by the hanging herb box. The edges of design parts round down in a cushioned effect and are separated only by a shallow trough. Again, and the herb box also shows this, the background may be cut entirely

52

through the wood in places to leave pierced openings.

The work of carving in deep relief begins to approach that of carving in the round. To be successful, the carver must be able to visualize the effect of full modeling and cut boldly to achieve it. The mere rounding over of edges and scooping of slight depressions in the raised parts of a design, no matter how deeply cut the background, will not give the desired result.

MATERIALS

While carving in relief may be done in either hard or soft wood, the material must be one which will allow the raised motifs to stand without danger of splitting off and one which will permit the kind and amount of modeling you want to give it. Small motifs and fine detail call for a close-grained hardwood. A raised design done in redwood will necessarily be broad and undetailed, such as the scroll patterns used on the wheelbarrow shown in this chapter. Choice of wood will be influenced by the use to which the piece will be put as well as the type of carving used to ornament it.

TECHNIQUE

The steps of carving in relief have been described in the chapter on how to carve. Repeated briefly, these consist first of making the vertical stop cuts around the entire motif, next making the slanting slicing cuts through the waste wood of the background down to the bottom of the stop cut. The remaining background wood is then cleared and the lowering and shaping of the standing parts, in other words, the modeling, is undertaken. All that remains to finishing the work is the refining of planes and outlines and smoothing background sections with light cuts made with sharp tools, care being taken to cut with the grain.

After even a brief carving experience, you will become aware of the importance of the several factors that add up to a good piece of relief carving. The choice of design as well as the way it will be carved should be influenced by the material used, whether hard or soft and whether the grain is close or coarse. The wood used should, in turn, be of sufficient strength and capable of taking the kind of polish and finish to suit it to the use to which it will be put, whether a rolling pin for holiday cookies or a fine cabinet.

The skill which you bring to the actual cutting of designs in relief is but one part of the fun of carving. Another is finding a ready use for the things you carve, uses fitting to the way we live now. While we can admire the masterly craftsmanship of ornate museum pieces, massively carved with birds and beasts, fruits, vines and the human figure, times and tastes have changed and we would have no use for such furniture even if we could make it! Instead, we will use our skills to make small household accessories, informal furniture, add to the architectural interest of our homes with our handiwork and make all the objects around us reflect our pleasure, be it but a wheelbarrow!

Before attempting an intricate carving in relief, try a simple pattern of interwoven straps such as this.

53

PROJECT NO. 9 • Case for an Oil Stone

You will get practice and later utility out of making this decorative case for your sharpening stone. The raised carving of stylized leaf pattern is simple to do and thoroughly modern in spirit.

Stock needed consists of two blocks of maple or other hardwood, each 5¾ by 2⅞ inches. Mortise both blocks inside to hold a hard Arkansas oilstone.

Leave the completed box unstained but protect the natural color of the white maple from oil discoloration by applying several coats of thinned shellac. Rub each coat after it is dry with pumice and a non-drying oil (e.g., automobile oil). The final coat is wax.

A finishing strop of natural cowhide may be glued to the bottom of the box.

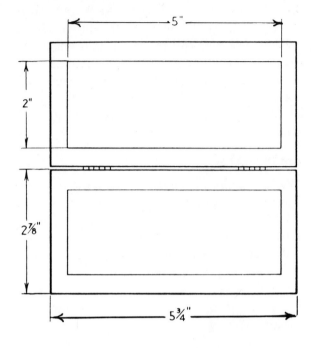

PROJECT NO. 10 • Spoon Holder

A collection of spoons becomes a decorative note in any room when hung on the wall in this small spoon holder. The drawer at the bottom will hold extras.

The holder shown was designed for small black-coffee (after-dinner) spoons; larger spoons would require some changes in the dimensions of the holder, but making it is still a simple project.

First, cut pieces to the size and shape shown in the drawing. Use a scroll saw to cut the curved pieces. Carve the drawer front before the drawer is assembled.

The slotted shelves fit into shallow grooves on the side pieces, but fit flush against the back section. Make the slots for the spoon handles by drilling two small holes and sawing to them.

Sand all pieces well, with the exception of the carving, and then join with glue and small finishing nails.

The wood used for this project is oak. The finish is a well rubbed and waxed stain of a medium brown to contrast with the silver of the spoons.

54

The hinges should be set in place while halves
of case are clamped together in alignment.

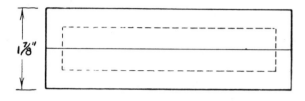

1⅞"

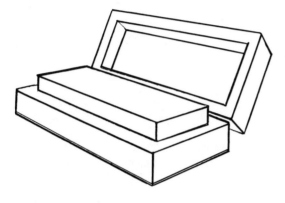

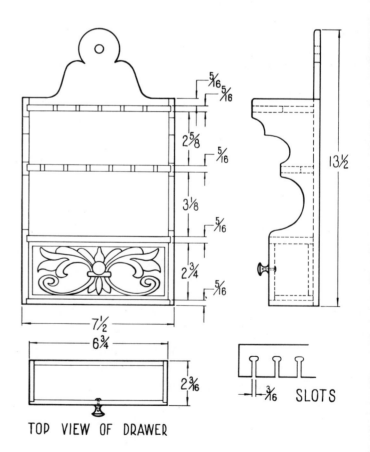

5⁄16 5⁄16

2⅝

5⁄16

3⅛

5⁄16

2¾

5⁄16

13½

7½

6¾

2³⁄16

TOP VIEW OF DRAWER

3⁄16   SLOTS

Stylized handshake design appropriate for guest book.

PROJECT NO. 11 • Book Cover

It's easy to make sturdy, long-wearing scrapbooks from wood. Wrapping-paper sheets or fillers can be purchased at the stationer's or "five-and-ten."

The wooden book shown, designed as a guest book, is appropriately decorated with a stylized handshake.

For the back cover and the backstrip of this book you will need ½-inch material, for the front cover ¼-inch stock. Only the front cover

is hinged. Double sheets of paper are held by cord laced through holes in the paper and the backstrip of the book.

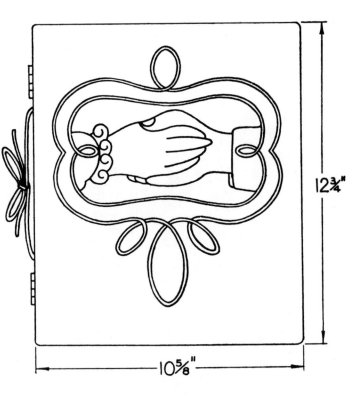

12¾"

10⅝"

Small vents in design permit
fragrance to escape.

PROJECT NO. 12 • Herb Box

If you grow herbs as much for fragrance as
you do for flavor, borrow this old Russian idea
and keep a bouquet of them in a hanging box
on the wall. Small vents—a part of the design
—allow the fragrance to escape into the room.
Any wood that may be carved is suitable for
this box. This one was made of red mahogany
with a natural finish.

First, cut all parts of the box from ½-inch
stock. Then lay out the carving design on the
front and side pieces. Drill the vent holes,
which are blacked in on the drawing, and then
file with a small three-cornered file or cut with
a jig-saw. Cut the carving lines to a shallow
V-groove.

The lid swings up on short dowel pins that are
fastened to the lid and put through holes in
the side pieces when the box is put together.
All joints are butt joints, held with glue and
finishing nails.

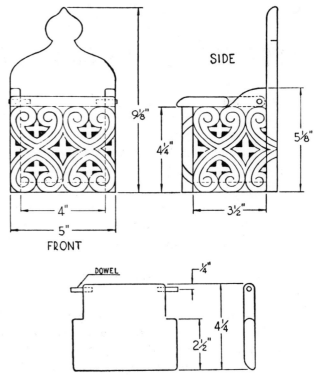

57

Chest open, showing hinged center board.
Tools on center board help hold others in place.

PROJECT NO. 13 · Carving Tool Chest

This partitioned chest is especially designed for a complete set of wood-carving tools plus such other wood-carving accessories as a mallet, sharpening stones, small clamps, and glue.

The chest is made of Philippine mahogany with brass corner plates, hinges, and hasp. The carving design is a variation of the traditional guilloche, pleasing to the eye and sufficiently intricate to make a fascinating carving project.

Divide the box into two equal halves. To insure accuracy, cut in half after building. The top and bottom form divided trays with identical partitions. Your larger gouges occupy these sections: one slightly larger section is reserved for the mallet, sharpening stones, and miscellany which require the full depth of the box. A small hook will hold the hinged board, which holds the smaller tools under a leather strap, when the chest is closed. Do not make this hinged board the full size of the box, but only large enough to cover the gouge sections. It serves the double purpose of holding lid-section tools in place when the box is closed.

Finish the mahogany chest with shellac and paste wax. Apply the shellac in several thinned coats, rub each thoroughly. Rub the final coat lightly with powdered pumice and non-drying oil. Then wax thoroughly.

58

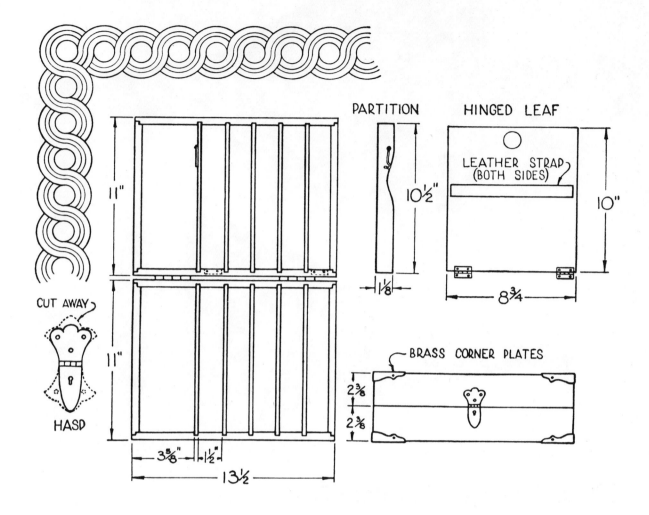

PARTITION

10½"

1/8"

HINGED LEAF

LEATHER STRAP
(BOTH SIDES)

10"

8¾

11"

CUT AWAY

HASP

11"

3⅝" 1½"

13½

BRASS CORNER PLATES

2⅜

2⅜

Dividing box in half on power circular saw.
Hand-saw may be used; requires more skill.

Corner plates can be home-made from brass
or bought at hardware or luggage stores.

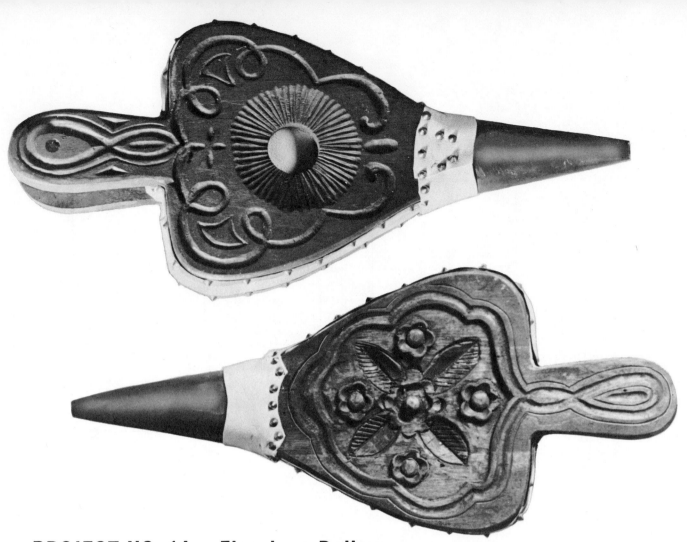

PROJECT NO. 14 • Fireplace Bellows

The materials you will need for this useful fireplace bellows are: two pieces of soft pine or hardwood suitable for carving (approximately 1 by 8 by 14 inches), a strip of soft leather about 24 inches long and 7 inches wide, a piece of light-gauge sheet copper 8 inches square, and some decorative upholstery nails and carpet tacks to complete the job.

Before they are carved, the two sides of the bellows are identical except that one has a 1½-inch hole bored in the center for the air intake and is about an inch longer than the other. Tack a leather flap over the hole on inner side, tacking at top of flap only. With a gouge cut a ½-inch trough in both pieces where they meet at the bottom to allow the air to escape. (See outlet detail.) Tack the leather to the curved shape of the bellows with a ½-inch overhang. The latter is turned back to cover the carpet tacks and held with additional decorative nails. (See detail of tacking procedure.)

Nail the spout, previously shaped to fit the already-rounded ends of the wooden bellows pieces, to the long side only. The fact that it is not solid on the other side is concealed and compensated for by the collar formed by the leather hinge, which is securely wrapped and tacked to the wood.

Stain the wood a dull brown. The leather is mellow white, and the copper spout and trim complete the color scheme.

The back and front views of bellows.
Hole in back is for air intake. A pointed, wooden
form will help shape the metal spout, which is soldered
at joint. Or have a metal-smith make it.

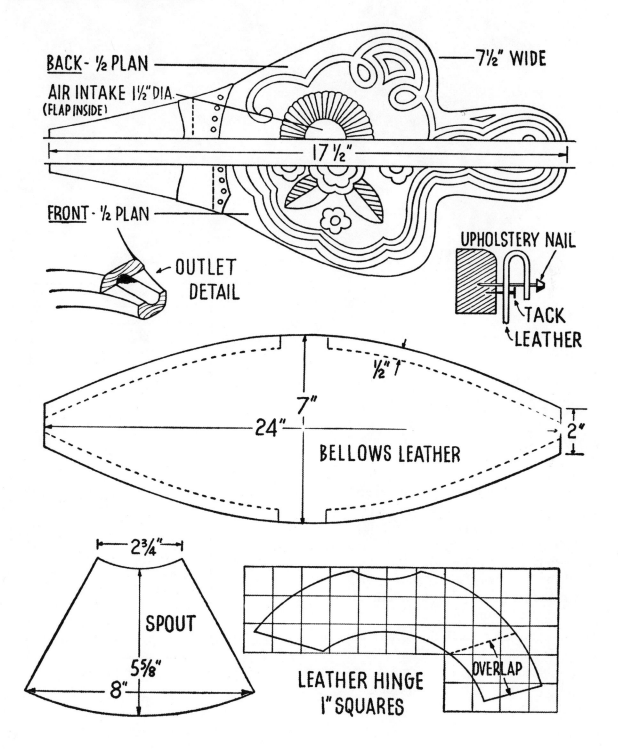

BACK- ½ PLAN

7½" WIDE

AIR INTAKE 1½" DIA.
(FLAP INSIDE)

17 ½"

FRONT- ½ PLAN

OUTLET
DETAIL

UPHOLSTERY NAIL

TACK
LEATHER

½" ↑

7"

24"

2"

BELLOWS LEATHER

2¾"

SPOUT

5⅝"

8"

LEATHER HINGE
1" SQUARES

OVERLAP

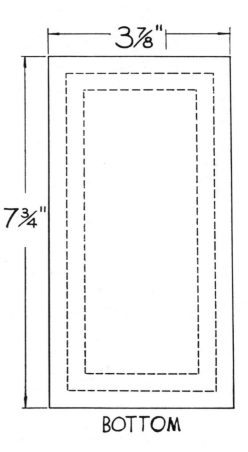

PROJECT NO. 15 •
Jewel Case

This small chest is planned in design and technique to require the simplest tools and little or no wood-carving experience. Although it is intended to hold jewelry, it will also keep cigarets handy on the coffee table. You should use wood that is somewhat soft—pine or Philippine mahogany, or a grade of oak that is light and corky in texture.

To make the box, first cut the lid, bottom, sides and ends from ⅜-inch stock and transfer the carving design to those parts you wish decorated. The first step in this type of carving is

3⅞"

7¾"

BOTTOM

62

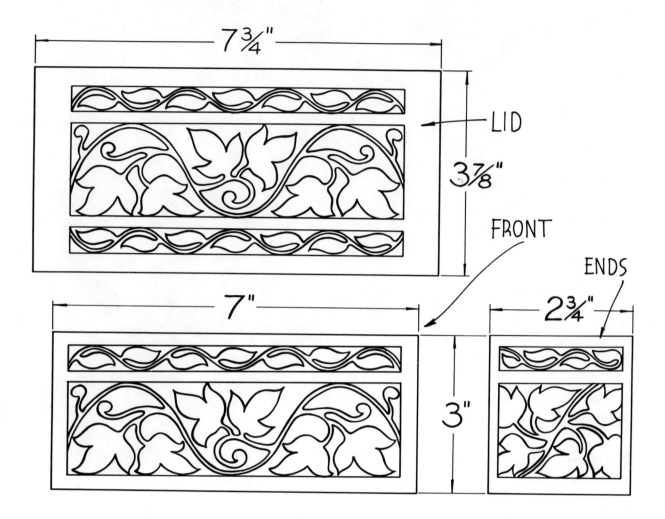

to sink all of the background area to a depth of about ⅛ inch with a small punch and a light mallet. Then round over the edges of the vines and leaves in the pattern with a sharp knife or chisel. Round over all edges of the bottom with a knife and finish with a wood rasp. Round the front and side edges of the lid in the same way. Join the sides and ends first and then fasten to the bottom of the box, letting the bottom project ⅜ inch on all sides. The lid overhangs an equal amount at front and sides but is flush at the back where it is fastened to the box with two small brass hinges. All joints are simple butt joints, held with glue and small brads.

If the chest is to hold jewelry, it should be lined. Cut pieces of light cardboard to the exact inside dimensions of the bottom, ends, and sides of the box and cover them with satin or velvet. Under the fabric you may put padding of sheet cotton. Draw the material smoothly over the side that will show and paste the edges down on the other side. Then slip these sections inside the box with or without glue. Finish the exterior of the box with oil stain. Then rub with wax.

PROJECT NO. 16 •

Garden Wheelbarrow

This sturdily built little barrow is decorative and can also take on many garden jobs. Loaded with pots of flowers, it could brighten many a corner in your garden or patio.

The handles are designed for a person 5 feet 5 inches tall or less. If you are taller, lengthen the handles accordingly.

The materials you will need are as follows: one carriage bolt ½ by 12 inches; two carriage bolts ½ by 2; two ½-inch pipe flanges; two 3-inch lengths of ½-inch pipe threaded one end; 1-inch redwood for panels; 2-inch stock for the frame; nails, screws, glue, and finish.

Begin by cutting a wheel 11½ inches in diameter from 2-inch stock. Drill a ½-inch hole at the center for the carriage-bolt axle. Screw pipe flanges at center on both sides of the wheel. Screw the short pieces of ½-inch pipe to the flanges to prevent side play of wheel. Flanges may have notches filed, as shown in the drawing, to make them more decorative. Coat both flanges and pipe with flat black metal paint.

Cut handle-chassis pieces and legs from 2 by 4-inch stock. Drill holes in handles at an 8-degree angle for the axle bolt and shape them as shown. A coarse wood rasp is useful in shaping the hand grip. Join legs and handles with a half lap joint, and bolt them together.

Form bottom, sides, and front panels from pieces of 1-inch stock glued together. Note that joined edges of bottom, front, and side panels are beveled to allow sides and front to spread from bottom to top. See drawing.

64

Pipe flanges joining redwood wheel, axle, notched to make them decorative.

Legs are joined to frame by half lap joints.

Transfer the carving pattern to the wood with carbon paper. Carve panels before assembling the barrow. First, stab outlines of design in the wood to a depth of about ¼ inch. Make these vertical cuts with gouges, varying the degree of curve and choosing tools which best fit the intricacies of the design. Gouge away the wood of the background areas to the depth of the stop cuts, and round over the edges of the remaining raised portions.

After carving, assemble the wheelbarrow. First, place the wheel. Then screw the bottom

boards to the handle-chassis pieces. Next, attach sides with screws so that outside surfaces are flush with outside edge of handle-chassis pieces. Fit the front section between sides and screw through the sides.

The wheel may have a tacked-on tire of a strip of old carpet or belting leather.

To finish, give the wheelbarrow two coats of penetrating oil seal finishing medium, which dries to a hard semi-gloss. It doesn't change the natural color of redwood, although the wood will eventually darken with age.

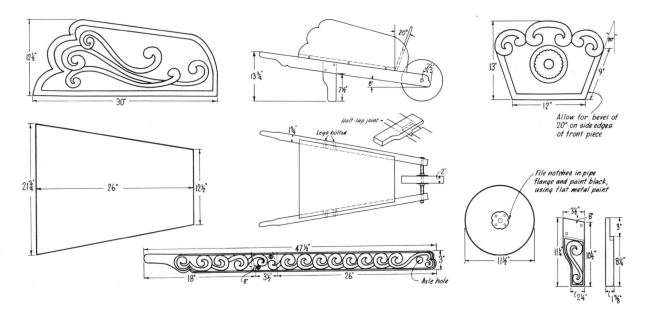

PROJECT NO. 17 • Dower Chest

The design and decorative carving motifs on this chest are based on an old Russian pattern. The crowned peacocks, of Byzantine origin, were often used as applied decoration by craftsmen of that country.

To make this chest, first dress the pieces for the corner posts and top and bottom rails to a square of 1½ inches. Then cut the corner posts to exactly 14 inches. Cut the rails 1½ inches longer than they appear on the surface

of the chest to allow for ¾-inch tenons at each end. These tenons are ¾ inch square, ¾ inch long, and ⅜ inch deep all around. Where they meet in the corner posts, they must be angled to form a miter.

You may cut tenons easily on a power circular saw, but they may also be made with a small backsaw. Next, cut the two stiles for the centers of the end sections. They are 1½ inches thick and 1½ inches longer than their fin-

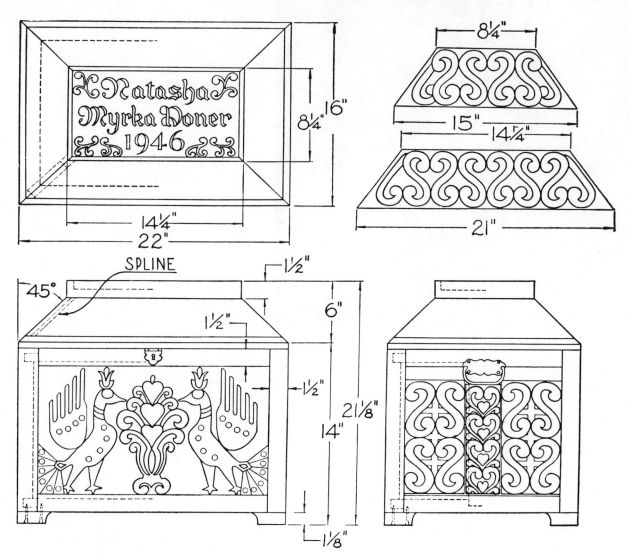

ished appearance. The tenons on each end are ¾ inch long and ⅜ inch deep on all four sides. Mark the outside faces of all pieces so that none will be cut "wrong side out." Then cut the mortises to receive the tenons on the corner posts. Mark and work with care so that the rails fit into the corner posts flush on all sides. Center stiles on the end rails and mark and cut the mortises.

Cut grooves ⅜ inch wide and deep in rails, corner posts, and stiles to hold the panels. In rails and stiles, the grooves run the full length and are easily cut on the circular saw, or again may be cut by hand with a combination plane or chisels. On the corner posts, the grooves stop in the mortise at each end.

The panels are ⅜ inch thick. You may have to glue the stock up to form the large front and back panels. Allow ⅜ inch all around on each panel to fit into the grooves in stiles and rails.

You are now ready to assemble the box part of the chest. Glue the parts and clamp together while the glue sets. While tightening clamps, test for squareness in all corners. The bottom is a piece of ⅜-inch plywood held by narrow strips glued and nailed to the lower rails.

Next, cut the frame for the lid section. Miter and dowel the corners. Bevel the top edges of this frame to a 45-degree angle as shown on the drawing. Cut lid panels to an exact fit on the beveled frame. Bevel top and bottom edges

Shallow-relief carving being done on a lid panel. The carving is done after pieces are cut.

of these to a 45-degree angle and then make the slanted miter cuts. This may also be done on a power saw with tilting table. If done by hand, you may set the pieces in a miter box and cut. Grooves, ¼ inch by ¼ inch, are cut in the faces of the miters to receive a thin spline across the corners. Use glue and small finishing nails to hold these pieces together.

Another frame, mitered and rabbeted, holds the panel on the top of the lid. When you have affixed this frame to the beveled panels from the inside with glue and nails and glued the top panel down, the lid section is completely assembled.

Next, fit the lid to lie perfectly on the box section and fit the hinges at the back. Center the handles on the stiles at the ends and a small hasp at the center front. All hardware on the chest shown is brass. The material used to make this chest is red cedar finished with rubbed waterproof varnish and wax to bring out the natural red tones of the wood.

Parts of chest, cut to size, carved, ready to glue together.

Hollowed out bodies of small hen and rooster allow them to serve as grain scoops or hold flowers or candies on the table. Material is redwood.

Carving in the Round

DEFINITIONS

Although all carving is sculpture—this being the "act or art of carving, cutting or hewing" —the word is usually reserved for statuary, a branch of sculpture treating figures in the round. For our purposes, the term carving in the round will refer to the cutting of any free-standing form entire in itself whether it is a whittled spoon or a totem pole hewn with an ax. Obviously it would be pretentious to call a scoop or ladle a sculpture, but it is just as obvious that these objects may appropriately be included in this section on carving in the round.

TOOLS AND MATERIALS

Equipment needed for carving in the round is much the same as that used for relief carving. The largest curved gouges are used for the roughing-out, the flatter gouges for surface finishing. In large work or where very hard wood is used, a larger and heavier mallet than that used in relief carving may be needed. Any wood, hard or soft, suitable for carving in general may be used for carving in the round. The choice of well-seasoned wood is important, however, because the large-sized pieces required for most carvings of this type will be prone to splitting and checking, particularly

69

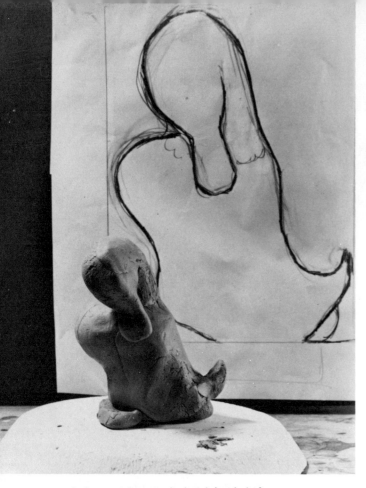

A clay model or rough sketch is a help for
the beginner when carving in the round.
A pencil outline for a small garden sculpture
has been developed from a clay model here.

Outline transferred to redwood block. Chalk outlines
indicate line of saw-cuts for removal of waste wood.

as stresses and strains within the block are
changed by removing sections of it and as new
surfaces reach the air. It may be necessary to
glue pieces of wood together to arrive at the
dimensions required for the piece in mind. If
so, take care to glue them with the grain going
in the same direction, to use a waterproof
glue, and to keep the whole well clamped together until the glue has completely set.

SPECIAL PROBLEMS

The greatest challenge in carving in the round
is the need for the ability to "see" a form in
three dimensions with the mind's eye and to
hold this form in the mind until it emerges
from the block. In any but the simplest projects this is no minor feat.

The beginner will find much help, both in
the planning and carving of a sculpture, in the
use of a small clay model. Use moist pottery
clay or plasticene and make several rough
sketches of your idea in one of these materials.
Do not refine or work long on these since they
are not to be copied exactly; indeed any attempt to do so is likely to lead to disappointment since clay is an extremely yielding
material, capable of much manipulation, and
wood is not. Moreover, modeling in a plastic
material and carving wood are opposing techniques.

Your model, then, is a reference for proportion and pose in the beginning steps of block-
ing-out the shape. It is also a means of "calling
your shots"—a preliminary note of your in-

70

Waste wood sawed away and block ready for roughing-in of shapes and planes. Note wood has been left for base.

Further waste wood is removed with a large curved gouge, cutting done across grain and around shapes. Chalk marks mark center lines and planes to be left high.

tentions. It is impossible, as well as undesirable, to copy a modeled piece of clay in wood, primarily because wood has grain, clay does not. The grain will speak and influence the shape of the simplest of wood forms, and for many sculptors of wood this is one of the most exciting of its features.

Having made a model in clay, the next step is to make pencil sketches of two or more sides of the model, enlarging them until they fit the proposed size of the material or until the size of the material desired is determined. When the pencil sketches are reduced to the simplest of outlines, these are transferred to the block.

With outlines on the block, it may be seen that there are sections of the wood that could be removed without interfering with the material needed for the form. If so, saw these away before beginning the work of carving.

Holding a large block, unless it is so large that it stands of its own weight, sometimes presents a problem. This can be solved in several ways. A board may be screwed to the bottom of the block with large screws, and the edges of the board then clamped to the bench. Since it may be desired to turn the piece on its side for some parts of the work, this may not work as well as a board provided with two large bolts or spikes that fit into corresponding holes hored in the bottom of the block. This allows the work to be lifted off the board at will. A board which could revolve, allowing the standing block to be easily turned, would be even more convenient.

71

Rough cross-grain cuts have been smoothed with flatter gouge cuts with the grain. Further finishing with files and sandpaper reveal graining of the wood— a factor which may influence the simplest of wood shapes.

Finished sculpture is rubbed and polished with several coats of oil to fit it for outdoor life. Note that size of base has been reduced from that of original block.

TECHNIQUES

It will be easier to carve from the top of a standing figure, working downwards. For this reason, a check on the direction of the grain before the block is mounted is a good idea. Direction of the grain is important in all work of carving in the round since any slender parts or projections must run along lengthwise of the grain, for they will surely break off if they go across grain. Delicate slender parts may be cut in hard, tough-grained wood if they lie along the grain and not across it, but they should not be attempted in soft wood. A closely knit design is preferable. Not only will it be less prone to breakage, it will be easier to carve and better suited to the spirit of wood.

When waste wood is removed around the outline of the piece, either by sawing or by cutting it away with gouges, the next step will be that of roughing in the various planes which give the piece its crude form. If this form is a bowl or spoon these planes are obvious. Even so, it will be surprising how much wood must be removed to hollow out a bowl, shape the handle of a spoon or round the forms of a small sculpture. This work should go fast, most cuts going across grain for rapid removal of wood. If a tool becomes buried, however, don't try to remove it with force. Instead, take another tool and cut the wood over it to set it free. The picture in the mind's eye must be looked at frequently as the shape emerges.

72

This fat porker in polished redwood is a model for a modern piggy bank.

Work around round forms until they closely approach the work of finishing. Finish cuts will be made with flatter gouges.

FINISHING

In relief carving you are advised against the use of sandpaper. Obliterating the tool marks would wipe out the charm of this type of modeling. This is equally true of some types of carvings in the round. There are instances, however, where the piece will be made more attractive or practical by polishing. Household utensils are often made more pleasing to the hand and easier to clean by filing and sanding them to a very smooth surface. The grain, if it proves interesting, can sometimes be brought into greater play in some sculptures with a highly polished finish. Be warned, however, that the work of polishing a piece may take as long as the carving of it, for if tool marks are to be removed they must all be removed, not just dulled or smeared.

Selection of a suitable oil or wax finish depends on the use of the piece. See the discussion in the chapter on finishes.

Finishing of the piggy bank model was speeded by the use of a power sanding wheel, possible because of blocky, plain surface.

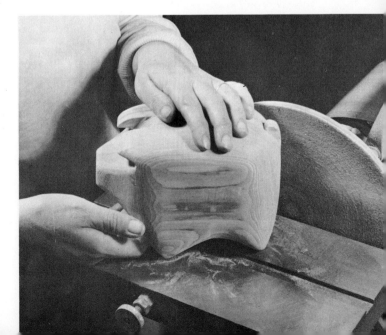

73

PROJECT NO. 18 •
Wood Spoon

Made from one piece of soft wood, ¾ inch thick, 2½ inches wide, and 9½ inches long, this spoon has many uses when properly finished with alcohol-proof varnish or lacquer. The outline and the pierced parts may be cut on a jig-saw or by hand. Or the spoon may be entirely hand-carved. Small three-cornered files will be useful in smoothing the hard-to-reach spots. Use sandpaper to round the spoon after it has been shaped with knife, gouges, and wood rasp—particularly for smoothing the braided section of the handle and shank.

PROJECT NO. 19 •
Spaghetti Forks

Like spaghetti, the idea for these carved serving forks with the perky handles came from Italy. Those shown were cut to outline on a power jigsaw, but they may also be cut out by hand with a scroll saw or whittled to shape. Use ⅜-inch stock of a fine-grained, tough hardwood such as cherry.

Draw the pattern to size on paper and transfer to the wood with carbon paper. Pattern must be laid on the wood so the grain runs lengthwise along the handle. Cut out the rough outline, then refine with a knife and round gouges.

Whittle edges round and reduce thickness of tines at the tip. An additional line of carving around the tines decorates the longer of the two forks. Smooth all parts with file and sandpaper.

Finish with clear lacquer or shellac. Allow finish to dry for several hours or overnight and rub smooth with fine steel wool.

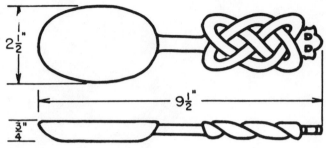

Easy-to-make serving accessory
is fashioned from one piece.

Additional decorative line is
carved around tines of larger fork.

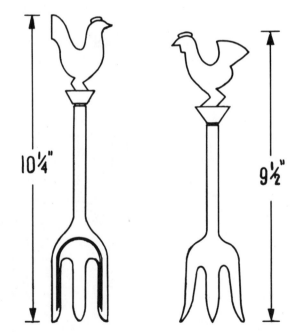

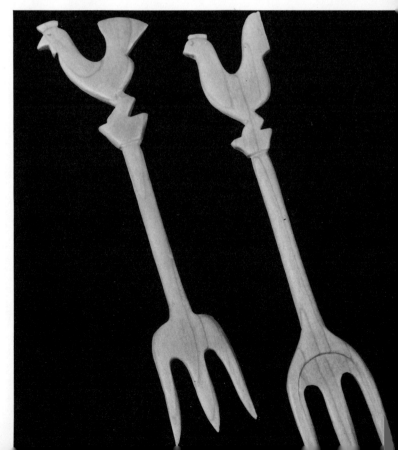

75

PROJECT NO. 20 •
Serving Dish

This double-duty fish made of cherry wood serves on one side as a divided dish, on the other as a chopping board. It is decorative on the kitchen wall, too.

All that you need to make one like it is an inch-thick piece of hardwood 11 by 14 inches, brace and bit, coping saw, and a few gouges.

Lay the pattern directly on the wood and saw around the outline. Then bore or saw out the hole. Begin carving by making vertical stop cuts around the ribs and eye.

Slope the dish sections from the outer edge to a depth of ⅜ inch at the center rib. Make vertical stop cuts along the lines in fin and tail and V-cuts along these lines. Round and smooth all edges with carving gouge or wood rasp. Sandpaper the entire fish, smoothing both sides and edges. Leave the chopping surface unfinished.

Apply several thin coats of waterproof varnish or lacquer to the dish side to make the wood resistant to spots and stains.

Hole prevents spilling chopped food.
Hold over a bowl when scraping
food off board.

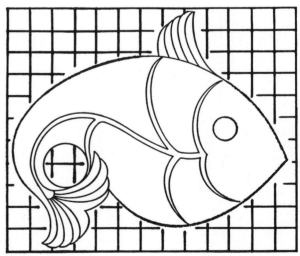

76

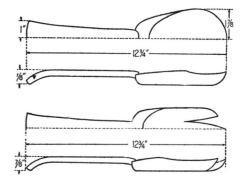

PROJECT NO. 21 •
Salad Set

The simple design of this large, useful salad set assures you of good balance in use. Stock is 1-inch mahogany or any other hard wood. Transfer the fork and spoon patterns directly onto the stock. Saw pieces to shape, and use inner lines as guides in carving. Begin carving each piece by hollowing out the inside of the bowl. Use a sharp gouge across the grain for rapid preliminary cutting, and finish by cutting with the grain. Note that the handle is raised and rounded where it meets the flat upper portion of the bowl.

After the top surface is carved, turn the piece over and round the bottom. Next, carve the bottom curve of the handle. Much of the work of shaping curves of the handle and bowl bottom can be done with a coarse file or wood rasp. Do the final smoothing with sandpaper. Finish with several coats of pure boiled linseed oil, rubbing between coats with very fine steel wool.

You get an idea of the giant size of these utensils from this photograph showing the artist's hands. She is carving spoon bowl.

PROJECT NO. 22 • Whittled Scoop

This whittled scoop is a good example of combined utility and decoration. Soft white pine is an excellent wood to use for carving this scoop, although any fine-grained, workable wood may be used. Several coats of clear varnish will make wood impervious to cold, mild heat, and liquids.

While it is possible to whittle the scoop from a solid block of wood, it is much simpler to start with a ¾-inch piece of stock for the handle and, with waterproof glue, join an additional piece to each side to gain the necessary thickness for the bowl.

Glue 1½-inch stock to each side of the ¾-inch piece the full length of the scoop. Before the side blocks for the bowl are added, jig-saw or otherwise cut to shape the handle design, drill holes, and cut away the wood inside the design that is to be removed. Cut the bowl roughly to shape with a band saw or with hand tools. Drill holes inside the bowl block to remove at least a part of the wood.

From this point begins the actual shaping of the scoop with gouges, knife, rasp, file, sandpaper. Finish, after thorough sanding, with water, pumice, and waterproof varnish.

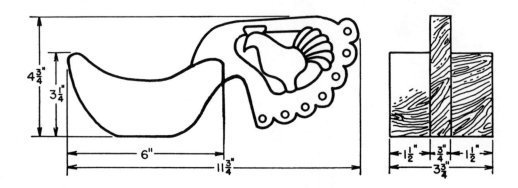

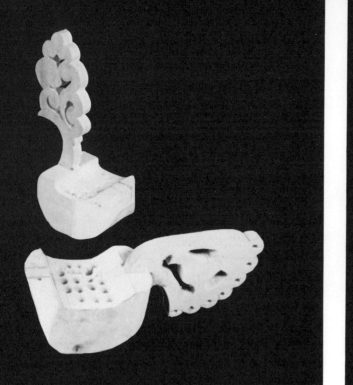
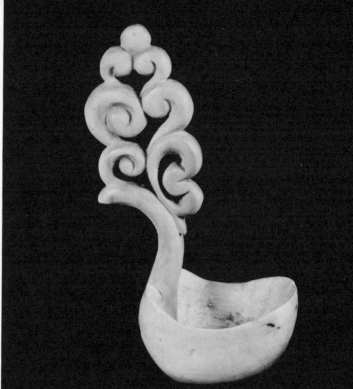

PROJECT NO. 23 • Wooden Dipper

Left. Removing wood from inside bowls is made easier by drilling many holes in the blocks.

Above. Completed dipper.

This dipper is easy to make from soft wood, using a few tools. Build up the block for the bowl by glueing additional pieces of wood to the ¾-inch piece which forms the handle and the center of the bowl. See procedure in making whittled scoop. Finish with varnish—sand lightly between coats.

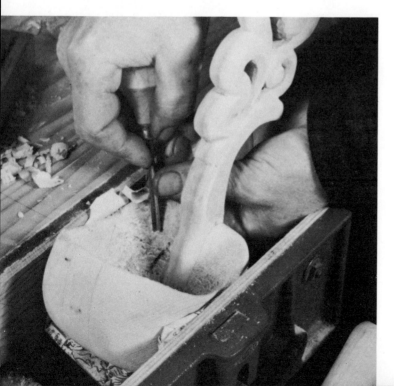

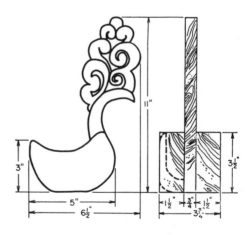

Above. Sketch of the built-up block.

Left. After drilling holes to remove wood inside bowl block, take remainder out with gouges.

PROJECT NO. 24 • Polenta Scoop

Flowers may lie in scoop without water, or a shallow pan might be fitted back into hollow.

Filled to overflowing with fruit, vegetables, or flowers, this sturdy wooden scoop is an attractive centerpiece for the table. It was inspired by the flour and polenta scoops of the Italian Tyrol.

You will need a block of straight-grained wood, approximately 4 by 6 by 14 inches, a hand saw, and a chisel. To make it, first draw the profile of the scoop directly on the block of wood. Then saw away the waste. Outline the top dimensions on the top of the block, and remove the waste wood around the handle with a saw.

Drill the handle and, with a keyhole saw, remove the wood to make the handhold. Cut the sides at an angle as indicated in the drawing. The back of the scoop is also cut on an angle. After the scoop has been blocked out, little remains for you to do but chisel the center portion into a hollow scoop shape. Round all edges with either chisel or wood rasp.

For high polish, use high-gloss varnish, rubbed to mellowness with powdered pumice mixed with a little non-drying oil.

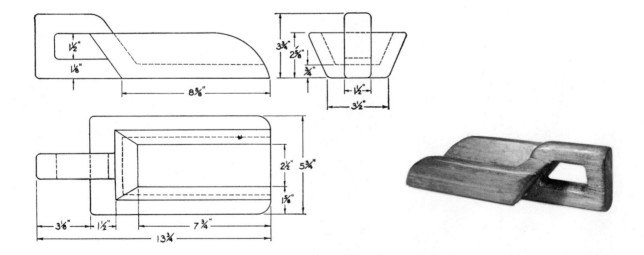

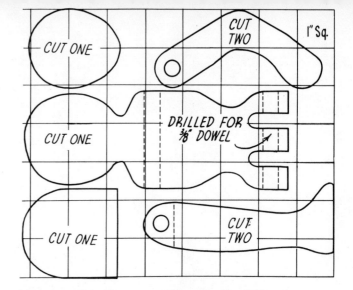

PROJECT NO. 25 •
Wooden Doll

Little girl dressmakers love to sew for a little girl doll such as this one. She is just the right size—11 inches—has a trim waistline and arms and legs that move, and is a "natural" blonde!

To make her you will need scraps of soft white pine or white cedar ¾ inch thick, two short pieces of ⅜-inch dowel, and a sharp "whittlin' knife." The features and shoes are painted with colored enamel over previously applied coat of shellac.

Begin by sawing out parts as shown on drawing. Drill ⅜-inch holes through shoulders and hips and at tops of arms and legs. Glue face and hair sections to either side of head section of body. Reduce thickness of wood at tops of legs to fit into slots at hips.

Whittle parts to shape by slicing chips from the square edges of the sawn-out parts. Note that while edges of body, legs, and arms are rounded and that arms taper to narrower dimensions at hands and that the head is well rounded, with hair and face defined, the doll as a whole retains a blocky, wooden character.

Whittled parts may be refined by further smoothing with files and sandpaper or with sandpaper only. When all parts are smooth, assemble by inserting dowels through arms and shoulders and legs and hips. Fasten dowel at either side of hips with small finishing nail and at front of each arm.

Shellac and sand with fine sandpaper before penciling and then painting on features and shoes.

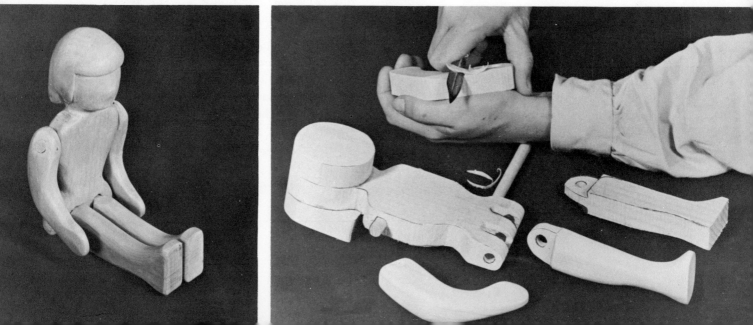

Oak chest with traditional designs adapted from the work of Spanish craftsmen.

Designs for Carving

CREATE YOUR OWN

It's easy, and gratifying, to design your own carving motifs. There are several ways to do this that will not call for freehand drawing, should you lack such ability.

Anyone, for instance, can draw a straight line along a ruler's edge and twirl a drawing compass to create geometric patterns, favorites of carvers for centuries. Squares, circles, diamond shapes and other geometric figures combine to make countless surface or border motifs. Chip carving designs, usually repeated arrangements of triangular shapes, are wholly geometric. Study pictures of collections of antique Spanish furniture for great variety in both pattern and application of geometrically designed forms. Illustrations in this book include a tray decorated with diagonal grooves and a tool chest ornamented with borders of interlocking circles. Both are ruler and compass designs.

Another approach to original design with no need for sketching skill lies in the use of scissors and paper. Who hasn't snipped paper folds to make "snowflakes" or rows of small children hand in hand? A fresh carving pattern for border or panel can be made in the same way. Use paper the full size of the planned section to be carved, fold and snip until you obtain a pleasing pattern. The simplest is usually the most effective; avoid intricacies which make a weak design and possibly one too complicated for good carving.

Problems of proportion for symmetrical objects, a spoon for instance, can often be solved by folding paper once down the middle and cutting an imagined one-half of the pattern actual size. Many of the Pennsylvania Dutch motifs appear to have been first designed in folded paper. Whether they were or not, they may be readily adapted to carving designs in this way. You will find them pic-

82

tured in books on the arts and crafts of early America as well as those concerned specifically with the handicrafts of the Pennsylvania Dutch.

Transfer paper cut-outs to the wood surface by drawing around it as it is held in place with cellulose tape.

A single shape, cut from light cardboard, can serve as a base for carving designs. The transfer of such a pattern is a simple matter, for outlining of the cardboard shape is done directly on the wood by drawing around the edge of the pattern. Use it in rows for borders; or use it to form one-half or one-quarter of a complete motif by placing it first right side up, then turning it over, etc., as required for symmetry.

Obviously, the methods just described will produce only flat patterns, but any design when carved in wood has raised and lowered sections that will reflect light and cast shadows. This effect of light on line and area within a wood-carving design is the final test of the worth of the chosen design. Yet a flat plan or pattern is essential as the first step in the design of any carved surface decoration, however derived. It will take imagination, experience, and study of actual carvings and photographic illustrations of carvings to develop the ability to choose the right design for carving and the best manner in which to carve it. One design may prove more vigorous when incised, another appear more striking when carved in relief. Before planning any ambitious carving it will be worthwhile to carve several experimental panels.

Carvings in the round are often inspired or planned by making "sketches" in modeling clay. These are usually made much less than actual size and are used primarily as a guide to proportions when blocking out the carved piece. Clay is mostly useful in producing mental suggestions. The contemplative pressing and pulling of this pliable and yielding material can bring forth fresh ideas which may be translated in wood if not literally copied. Again, imagination and the ability to hold the desired total effect firmly in the mind's eye are of first importance.

Border designs in variety may be planned
by using a single cardboard shape,
cut out and drawn around with pencil.

83

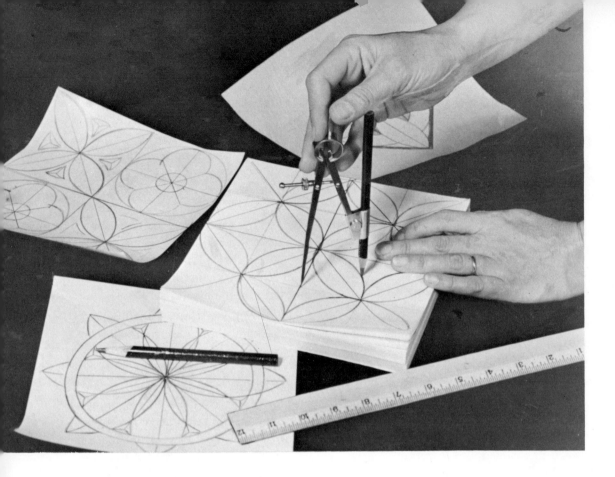

It's easy to make geometric designs with drawing compass and ruler, such designs form a base for many carving patterns.

ADAPTING TRADITIONAL MOTIFS

As you observe actual carvings and pictures of carvings, you will notice that certain motifs, with much variation but essentially the same, appear again and again through many different periods of furniture and architecture. The undulating vine, the flowing band of interlacing circles or scrolls (called a "guilloche" and said to be found in all styles since the Assyrian), the linen-fold and cartouche, derived from paper or cloth curls and folds, these and many more are the classic carving patterns. They have been used because they are tested decoration and very possibly because they are pleasurable to carve.

If these traditional designs appeal to you, look for them in museums and pictured collections of antique furniture in books and magazines. Make sketches and compass and ruler drawings and keep notebooks and scrapbooks for inspiration in use of this type of motif.

The problems in using classic patterns are those of selecting motifs that will combine when more than one is used on a piece and of adapting them to suit modern tastes and to fill the spaces to be carved. In combining motifs, strive to use those related in scale and spirit to arrive at a harmonious whole. Usually, you will want to use fewer different designs on the same piece than were used in times past. You will also want to simplify the individual design units, subtracting extra flourishes or extraneous figures. In adapting designs to space, use the paper cut-outs and cardboard shapes described as methods of creating your own designs.

COPY PUBLISHED DESIGNS

Line drawings of carving designs which deco-

84

rate specific craft projects are often printed in books and magazines. This book features a number of these. Such projects are published for the purpose of copying and many of the carving designs are printed over squares to make this easy. When the scale of the squares is indicated as ½ inch or 1 inch, merely draw lines to make a corresponding number of squares of that size and fill in the outlines of the design within the squares, just as they appear within the original square. Where no squares have been printed, trace the drawing and draw lines over it to form small squares. To enlarge to fit your exact space, make the same number of squares over it of whatever size they may turn out to be, and proceed to fill in outlines as they appear in the small squares over the original. This can be done with any line drawing to enlarge but retain its original outlines and proportions.

OTHER DESIGN SOURCES

The practiced eye will see designs that may be adapted to wood carving throughout the whole field of design. They may appear on wallpaper, fabrics, wrought in iron or woven in lace. No matter what the source of a possible wood-carving design, it must be, or be made to be, suitable to the character of wood and chisel and gouge techniques. This usually means that it will have, or be built up to have, a boldness and strength to make a decisive pattern. Areas must be definitely bounded, for a line that fades out or trails off hazily, while pleasing in a pencil sketch, cannot be stated well in wood. The best designs will "move" or flow without uncomfortable interruptions, or appear in well-related units without giving a spotty or broken appearance.

Collections of published handicrafts of peasants of Europe, those of our own early settlers, magazine illustrations, including those in the advertising sections, and contemporary crafts books will all prove good sources of wood-carving designs. A seeking, discerning eye will find them everywhere.

Experiment with the kindergarten technique using folded paper and scissors—this will produce unlimited patterns and ideas for possible carving.

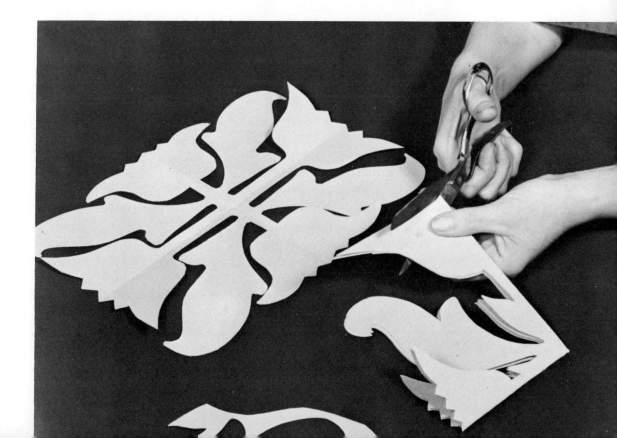

85

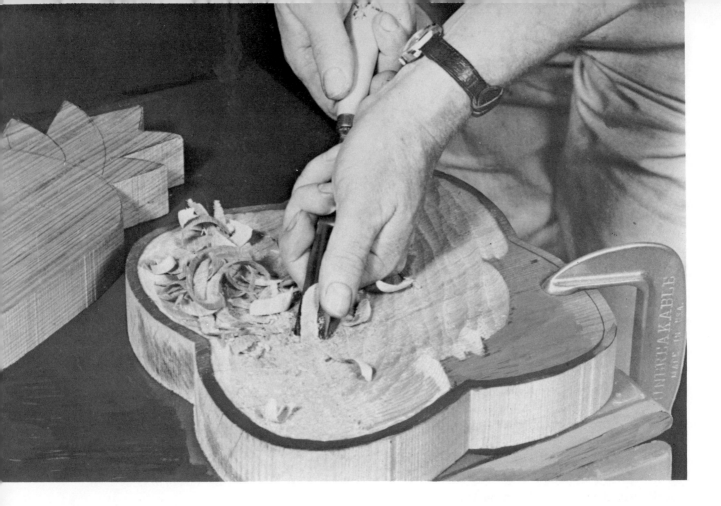

Work of cutting softwood goes rapidly.
Here, the hollow of a fruit bowl is being scooped
out with a large gouge cutting across grain.

Woods for Carving

HARDWOODS AND SOFTWOODS

According to the lumber dealer, those woods that grew as trees which shed their broad leaves in winter are the hardwoods. The softwoods are those that come from the coniferous, needle-leaved evergreens. It can be seen that this is a botanical classification rather than one of actual characteristics, especially when it is noted that the very soft basswood is thus a hardwood and the hard, tough-fibred fir is a softwood. As the wood-carver is interested first in the degree of actual hardness under the tool, he is accustomed to refer to woods as hard softwoods, medium-soft hardwoods, medium-hard hardwoods, hard hardwoods, etc.

SELECTING WOOD FOR CARVING

Since wood which will carve easily and well and wood so knotty and tough that it is impossible to carve can come from the same tree, it is necessary to choose the pieces of stock for a project by examining it. In most cases, stock with the straightest grain and the least striping of color, since a change in color may mean a change in hardness, and the fewest and smallest knots will be the best choice. Test it with your thumbnail to get some idea of the hardness.

Attempting to select wood by name alone is often futile since one general name may cover a dozen varieties. Unfortunately, woods do not carry labels and there is no guarantee that

86

all oak, for instance, will carve well, although oak has long been a favorite carving wood. Oak is a medium-hard or hard hardwood with a tough, springy grain which will not break off easily, making it particularly suited to bold raised designs in traditional styles. Japanese or Siberian oak is of good temper, although some may have spongy streaks in it. It is medium-hard.

The familiar red cedar used in cedar chests is but one kind of cedar; the name actually applies to many aromatic softwoods. "Cigar box" cedar, more properly known as Spanish cedar, is quite soft and excellent for chip carving and all incised carving. Port Orford cedar, the most aromatic of all, is white or yellowish white and a delightful whittling wood.

White sugar pine is easily whittled and carves well, providing tools are very sharp so they cut but do not bruise or mash the soft fibres.

Redwood is slightly harder than pine. The lovely color, good texture, and unexacting requirements of this wood make it very pleasant to carve. Selected pieces will hold broad detail in relief carving; much of it is excellent for incised carving, chip carving, and carving in the round. Since it weathers well and resists decay, it is a suitable wood for pieces to be left out of doors.

Philippine mahogany, a medium-soft hardwood, is another good wood for the beginner. It is of an attractive reddish-brown color and is quite uniformly carveable. It is no relation to the true mahoganies. Of these, the Honduras and Cuban varieties are the best for carving.

Walnut, too, is a fine and choice wood; avoid pieces with a highly decorative grain. Cherry is another richly colored wood which may prove somewhat hard but which carves well with sharp tools and holds fine detail.

Beech, birch, butternut, and maple are all good for kitchen accessories and table and serving ware, because they have a light color that takes a beautiful natural finish, are hard

This turned box decorated with incised carving is made of myrtle, a hardwood of light tan color. Box lid and base are stained black.

enough to resist abrasion and wear, and have no taste or odor. Butternut is a medium-soft hardwood; beech, birch, and maple are hard hardwoods. In fact, some maple is extremely hard and not recommended for carving at all. Western varieties are softer than eastern.

In general, the close-grained woods should be chosen for carving with fine detail and for any piece which must take a fine, hard finish because of the use to which it is to be put. The coarse-grained woods are best used for carvings done in a broad, free manner and for those that have less exacting demands of use and finish.

SOURCES OF WOOD FOR CARVING

In the beginnings of carving practice it is natural to sieze upon the wood immediately available, be it a box end or scraps left from building construction. As skill develops you will want worthy material for your carving projects. Your best source of material will be the lumber yard in your community which makes a practice of tossing short pieces, odds and ends of all kinds of wood in one special place. Here you can learn to recognize kinds of wood, find the little piece you had in mind for a special project or a piece that will inspire another. It is just the place for the craftsman who often is unable to say just exactly what it is he does want!

All the wood that comes to the carver will not come from the lumber yard. Old and massive furniture, no longer fashionable or useful, will provide good wood to carve, not only because it was of a quality deemed good enough for furniture to begin with but because it is sure to be dry. Well-seasoned wood is to be desired but often hard to find. Lack of proper season-

ing is the main fault of wood which you might acquire from felled fruit trees or windfalls.

Because fruitwoods in general are so pleasant to carve, you might save some pieces for small carvings in the round, if you are willing to gamble on the chance that these will not check and split, as they often do.

Driftwood is a source of wood for the carver who is willing to take a chance with his tools and who doesn't mind continual sharpening. The inevitable sand and grit ground into this wood is hard on tools, but occasionally a piece of driftwood is found of such lovely color and texture that it is definitely tempting.

We have not discussed rare or exotic woods here because they are not readily available and are expensive. Should they interest you, you will find advertisements of mail-order suppliers of such woods and offers of sample collections and catalogues in the pages of magazines devoted to the woodworking crafts or crafts in general.

Lamp bases of Primavera, a medium-hard hardwood, pale yellow in color and therefore sometimes called "blonde mahogany".

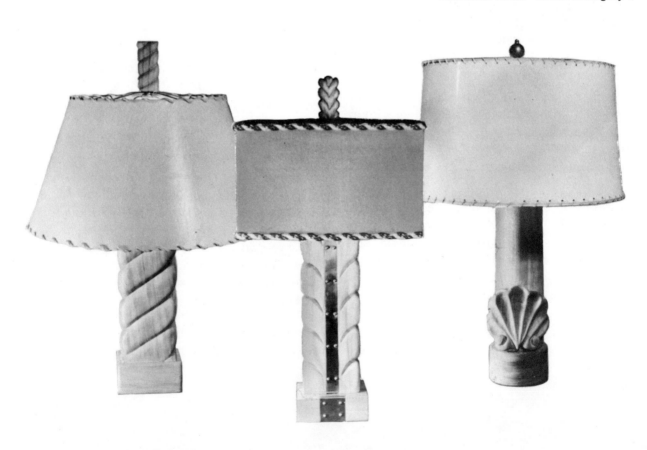

Garden furniture and carved pieces to be placed out of doors should be protected with coats of raw linseed oil or other oil seal for exterior use.

Finishes for Carvings

THE FINISHING TOUCH

The first aims of the wood-carver in applying a finish to a carving are to enhance and preserve the full effect of his carving, to preserve and bring out the full natural beauty of the wood, and to fit the piece to the use to which it will be put. The first two parts of this three-fold aim make several of the common treatments given wood in other branches of woodworking impractical or even fatal to carvings, while the latter part presents special problems.

The type of carving enters into the question of finish as well. No abrasives, sandpaper, or steel wool should be used on carving that depends for the best effect on the tool cuts. Nor is it advisable to use grain fillers because they clog grain or tool marks. Bleaches or water stains must also be avoided as these raise the grain and undo the natural polish of tool cuts. Oil stains may be used to color the wood; and to preserve it, linseed oil may be rubbed into it with a soft cloth, allowed to dry, and polished

with several light coats of furniture wax. Modern trends in wood finishing are towards preserving natural wood color rather than disguising it with colored stains. It is sometimes desirable, however, to enrich the natural color very slightly or to tone down light-colored streaks in it by mixing a small amount of burnt umber powder with small amounts of turpentine and linseed oil. Color can be lightened by rubbing excess oil away before it dries or darkened by adding more coats.

Large pieces, such as garden sculptures or furniture, are prone to checking and should be given frequent coats of slow-drying raw linseed oil, well rubbed into the wood. Use boiled linseed oil and furniture wax on pieces that will live more protected lives.

Obviously, salad bowls and serving dishes cannot be finished with anything as smelly and unappetiizng as turpentine, linseed oil, or furniture wax! If a satiny natural finish is desired for bowls, plates, or scoops to be used with cold foods, these may be rubbed with

Avoid finishes which might taint food when finishing buttermolds, salad bowls or other baking and serving utensils of wood. Instead use beeswax, or edible oils. Long use provides the best polish for these useful items.

Enamels in gay colors are used on this little pull toy for a toddler. Wood of the chassis has been left natural under coats of clear shellac.

Mane, tail and hooves of this toy horse are enameled a shiny black for contrast to the light yellow paint of the body. Paint on the body was wiped to reveal wood grain before paint was dry. The whole was sealed when dry with shellac.

90

beeswax shaved into mineral oil and melted over hot water. Repeated applications of olive oil during the life of kitchen ware will give it a nice patina. Neither the beeswax nor the olive oil finishes will prove sufficient protection against grease marks or hot liquids. To successfully withstand either, woodenware must have a tight coat of one of the waterproof spar or "bar" varnishes or lacquers applied according to the directions on the container.

For special effects it is sometimes desirable to brush colored house paint or thinned enamels over a carved piece, wiping it off with a soft cloth before it has time to dry but has set slightly. This will leave a light residue of color in the grain of the wood and often gives an added feeling of texture, particularly in the coarse-grained woods.

When the wiped paint is dry, the surface can be sealed with wax or coats of thinned shellac. In using shellac it is well to remember that this clear finish is not waterproof and that no great demands of wear or durability should be made on it. Several thin coats—the thinner used should be alcohol—are much better than a single thick coat. The clear varnishes and lacquers are much better protective coats but require spraying on, not brushing, for the best results.

Occasionally carved or whittled pieces, such as the toys shown in this chapter, are fashioned for the ultimate pleasure of a child rather than for the beauty of the carving or the wood, and these can be made more attractive by painting them with bright enamels. Do not give painted toys to tooth-cutting infants. Paint manufacturers decline to label their product as containing stomach poisons on the grounds that paint isn't food, but a few modern paints contain poisonous ingredients in minute amounts. To be on the safe side, toys for the very, very young should have only a natural finish.

CARE OF CARVINGS

Wood can literally starve to death if natural oils are not replaced as they dry out. Prolonged wetness is hard on it too. It can be protected from both damp and dry climates by an occasional coating of oil. An oily furniture polish is usually all that is needed for carved furniture. If it becomes dirty or inclined to feel sticky, go over the piece with a soft cloth wrung out in very hot water, dry, and polish with linseed oil thinned with a bit of turpentine, or use furniture oil, or paste wax.

Table and kitchen utensils may be given a quick swish through hot soap suds and dried immediately but they shouldn't be allowed to soak in water. An occasional rubbing with one of the edible oils, mineral oil, beeswax or paraffine wax is good upkeep for them.

CHOOSING HARDWARE

Locks, lockplates, hinges, handles, bolts, and similar hardware items may be spoken of as a part of the finish of a carved piece, but in some cases they should be considered in the first planning. A properly placed flat surface must be reserved on the front of a chest, for instance, for the lockplate, and this, in turn, should be thought of in relation to the carved design.

The ornate looking hinge on this salt box was made by adding two half-circles of light sheet iron cut to shape as an over-lay on the flaps of a common hinge.

An antique lockplate of wrought iron such as this one should inspire a very special piece of carving.

The proper choice of hardware can add much to both function and appearance of your carvings. Where they will be concealed, function will be the only consideration and items to be had at any hardware counter will serve. If you want a secure lock, an efficient modern one can hide behind a hand-made lockplate; and a heavy lid of a chest should have the support of smooth-working lid lifts. In the matter of appearance on exteriors, most modern hardware fails in charm or character suitable to wood carvings. One exception is marine hardware. A landlubber who feels that his carved treasure deserves the finest polished brass fittings should shop for them at the ship chandler's.

Fine reproductions of iron hardware in period designs, as well as some brass ones, are made by New England craftsmen. These are mostly of the style known as Colonial. Some Spanish-type iron hardware is made in California and New Mexico. Look for advertisements and offers of catalogues from all of these sources in the pages of home-decorating magazines.

The antique-hound can strike a fresh trail in going after old hardware, and while it is rare, it is to be found and worth hunting. A pair of interesting hinges or a fascinating lock might inspire a prize carving!

It is also possible to adapt standard hinges by adding an overlay of light sheet brass, copper, or iron and cut faceplates for locks of these materials. Use cold chisels to cut iron, metal snips for brass or copper. File edges smooth and drill holes for screws.

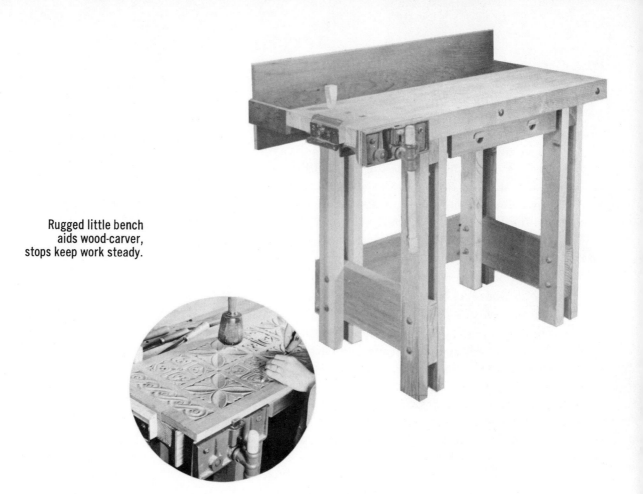

Rugged little bench
aids wood-carver,
stops keep work steady.

Wood-carver's Workbench

While this small workbench was designed for a wood-carver, it is large and strong enough for general craft use. A shallow tray at the back of the work surface keeps tools and patterns ready for use but out of the way.

To build it, use dry, seasoned lumber. Douglas fir is suitable. You need 2 by 4's for top and legs and upper leg braces; 2 by 8's for lower leg braces; 1-inch stock for drawer, lower back rail tray, and tray back; plywood for drawer and pulls.

Power tools are helpful, but all of the work can be done with hand tools. You need saw, hacksaw, hammer, screwdriver, brace and an assortment of bits, plane, and wrench.

You should adjust the bench height to fit the person who will use it. The work surface should be approximately on a level with the user's hip bone. This saves bending and helps prevent fatigue.

To hold work firm without clamps, equip the bench with bench stop, adjustable pegs, and a woodworking vise. If you have the vise before you build the bench, any necessary mortising or fitting can be done as you go along. Other hardware includes: 12 machine bolts, $\frac{3}{8}$ by $5\frac{1}{2}$ inches; 3 carriage bolts, $\frac{1}{2}$ by 16 inches; number 12 flat head wood screws, $2\frac{1}{2}$ inches long; lag screws, $\frac{3}{8}$ by 6 inches; and one hanger bolt for the T-hinge which forms the folding bench stop on the left end of the bench.

93

MAKING THE TOP

Build the top first. Select ten 2 by 4's, each approximately 50 inches long, and dress them to 1½-inch thickness. Lay the pieces side by side on edge with grain running the same way. Draw a center line across the top and lines 4 inches in from each end. Carry all three lines down one side of each piece and locate middle point. Drill ½-inch holes at each point as in the detail below.

Counterbore the hole at left front to keep bolt head out of the way when mounting vise. Counterbore all holes on the back side of the top section to take carriage bolt nuts.

The top is glued and bolted together. Slide the 16-inch carriage bolts through the first piece and coat the inside surface of the piece with glue. Coat sides of the next piece with glue and slide it over bolts. Continue until all 10 pieces are fastened together and then tighten the bolts slightly. Tap the top level with a block and finish tightening the bolts with a socket wrench. Wipe off excess glue, square the ends, and cut the section to its finished 48-inch size. To finish, cut bolts off flush and plane surface smooth.

LEGS

Cut and dress the legs and leg braces. Sandwich braces between double 2 by 4 legs and bolt legs and braces together with machine bolts. Use screws to fasten the back rail, a piece of 1 by 8-inch stock, to the back of the legs in line with the side rails.

To assemble the bench, turn the top upside down, with carriage-bolt heads to the front. Center the legs on it with the front of the legs 1½ inches behind the front of the top. Drill through the upper leg braces and into the top. Anchor legs to top with lag screws.

ACCESSORY EQUIPMENT

Make the tool tray and back stop of 1-inch material. Fasten the tray to the legs with screws and screw the back stop to the back legs and tray edge.

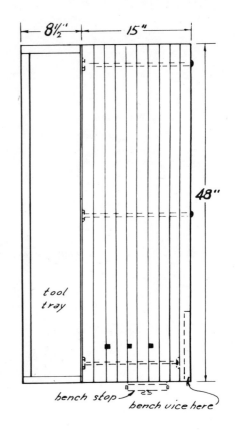

Above. Ten 2 by 4's, dressed, glued, and bolted together, make large, sturdy bench top. Kept in tray, tools and patterns do not clutter work space.

Right. To save bending, build bench at height most convenient for you. Woodworking vise, bench stop, movable peg optional. They hold wood firm, leave hands free.

94

Install the vise next. It may be necessary to cut the thickness of the top to 2 inches on the left end for this installation. Next, cut 3 holes in the bench top and fit a peg for them.

The bench stop is a large T-hinge faced with hardwood. The leg of the T is screwed to the underside of the bench.

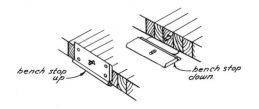

When the stop is up, a hanger bolt (a headless bolt with lag-screw point) passes through a hole in the wood facing. The hinge is held in place with a wing nut. When not in use the stop may be loosened so that it drops out of the way.

DRAWER

Make the drawer box 3½ by 14 by 12¼ inches with butt ends at the back and rabbet joints at the front. Fit with a plywood bottom. Nail

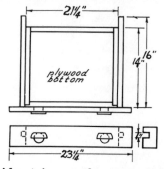

1-inch guide strips on the upper sides to slide the drawer. Nail matching runner strips 16 inches long to upper side braces of the work table so that the drawer when closed will be flush with the legs. Face front of drawer with a strip 3¾ by 23¼ inches. Bore holes 1½ inches in diameter and partially cover with pieces of plywood to form pulls.

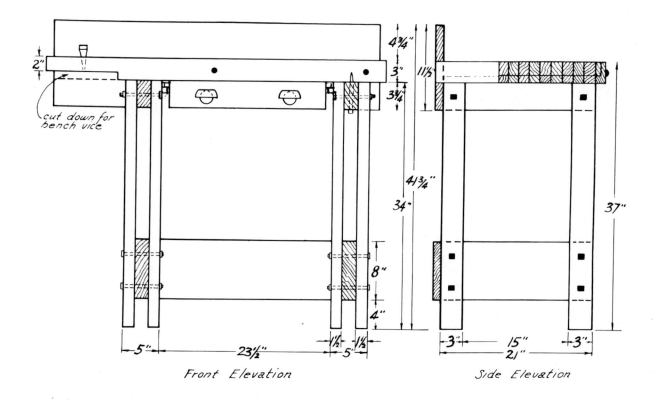

Front Elevation   Side Elevation